WHERE IS MY FATHER?

John Job

WHERE
IS
MY FATHER?

Studies in the Book of Job

MOORLEY'S Print & Publishing
23 PARK ROAD, ILKESTON, DERBYS, DE7 5DA · ENGLAND

ISBN 0 86071 409 8

Enquiries should be addressed to:
Moorley's Print & Publishing
23 Park Road
Ilkeston
Derbyshire DE7 5DA

Printed in Great Britain by
Redwood Books, Trowbridge, Wiltshire

CONTENTS

ACKNOWLEDGEMENTS

Many will suspect that it was the fascination of a namesake that prompted this book. But the truth is that it owes its origin to the fact that students at Immanuel College, Ibadan, had Job as their main Old Testament assignment for their second year. What follows here is indebted to their interest. But I am grateful too for the encouragement of Professor A.S. Herbert, who read the first draft of the book, to my former Cliff College colleague, Dr A.S. Wood, who advised me at a late stage, and to the Methodist Publishing House and its Readers, who made helpful suggestions for the first edition.

The book has now been rescued from oblivion in this new edition by Moorley's and I am grateful that the continuing demand will be met.

Bedford   JOHN JOB
December 1993

INTRODUCTION

Any minister thinking back over his experience of pastoral work is likely to agree that the sufferings of his people (apart from those inflicted by himself, which no doubt show a contrasting measure of predictable uniformity) are strangely apportioned. The most considerate husbands and wives sometimes have the most difficult partners. The wisest parents can have the most irresponsible children. Those who seem least in need of testing or maturing are those for whom the burden of trouble seems to be unfailingly present. There are families to which Providence seems to mete out such an outlandishly unfair share of problems that it is not uncommon to hear people mutter, 'Everything happens to them'. Moreover physical suffering and misfortune figure high on the list of such problems, as in the book that we are about to study.

The Book of Job is not the first contribution to a discussion of this difficulty. Research has yielded no less than seven works from Egyptian, Babylonian and Sumerian sources whose theme is comparable. All of them come from a period long prior to the earliest possible date for Job, and their existence shows how the problem of human suffering and its relation (or lack of it) to merit has exercised a fascination for writers from the very dawn of literary activity.

But it is to the Book of Job that a Christian will naturally turn for light on this subject. It is by no means the only place in the Bible where the question is treated. One thinks in the Old Testament of the story of Joseph, of Psalms 49 and 73, of the so-called Servant Songs in Isaiah, particularly 52:13–53:12. And the New Testament too deals with the theme, both with reference to the undeserved sufferings of Jesus himself and (for instance, in Romans 5:3–5) from the point of view of Christians. But it is to the Book of Job that one must turn for the most thoroughgoing investigation the Bible affords.

Yet this book is far from being an easy one to understand. This is certainly true as far as the line by line details of the Hebrew text are concerned. One of the reasons is the unusually large measure of textual uncertainty, scarcely matched in any other biblical book. A connected problem is the great number of rare words, whose meaning has often to be inferred either, for lack of parallel from the passages where they occur in 'Job' itself, or from appearances of the root in the literature of cognate Semitic languages.

Then there is the question whether, quite apart from copyists' errors, the Book of Job, as we have it, is anything like the book as it left the hand of the original author. Some scholars think that the beginning and end of the book once existed as a self-contained narrative, and that the dialogue was added later. Further suspected additions are the poem on Wisdom in Chapter 28 and the whole section of Elihu's speeches (Chapters 32–37), while others doubt whether the double speech in the mouth of God is likely in its entirety to have been an original feature (cf. 38:3, 40:7).

Finally, there is a problem which stands mid-way between those which can be ascribed to deliberate editorial activity and those which arise from faulty transmission of the text. This lies in the fact that the third cycle of speeches is incomplete, with no contribution from Zophar. It is arguable moreover that some of the verses ascribed to Job in this section are not easy to interpret in the light of his general standpoint, and as a result various attempts have been made to reconstruct this part of the book.

To some extent it is true that matters of importance hang on the validity of such theories, and some further mention of these possibilities will be necessary. But in general, the position adopted here is that, regardless of the process by which the Book of Job came to be as it is, the expositor's basic task is to elucidate the work as we have it, regarding the author of it as the one who put it into its present form, keeping an open mind in areas where subsequent accidental dislocation is suspected, but not despairing too easily of making sense of what appears, say, in the New English Bible, which, with a few minor exceptions, translates the text in the order of the Hebrew.

There is no dearth of excellent commentaries which deal in detail with such matters as are discussed in the foregoing paragraphs. H. H. Rowley records hearing a lecture in which that by E. Dhorme was voted the finest in any language on any biblical book,[1] a verdict which scholarly caution all but allows him to endorse. His own should probably rank in any bibliography as the most helpful to the widest range of readers.[2] Best buy, if still obtainable in the second-hand market, is the unpretentious century-old contribution of A. B. Davidson to the Cambridge Bible for Schools and Colleges. And for a fine brief commentary, Francis Andersen's contribution to the Tyndale series deserves mention—a book which regrettably appeared too late to be fully reckoned with in this present study.

But our purpose here is to write something different from a commentary. Perhaps the position can be compared with that of a visitor to an art gallery. He sees a great painting there. He looks at it from a distance, and receives an overall impression. He moves up close and examines the brushwork, studying the artist's execution of the various parts of his painting. Of course, these two approaches interact, and one contributes to the effect of the other. But it does seem undeniable, as one looks at books available on Job, that it is help in the area of total understanding that is most urgently needed. When the most hopeful emendations have been adopted, when the most likely construction has been put on the difficult lines, what is it that the Book of Job contributes to the understanding of man's predicament? Is it a quaint relic from an alien culture and bygone days? Or does it, when we reach the heart of its message, offer answers as fresh and as relevant as the one o'clock news?

[1] In the prefatory note to E. Dhorme, *The Book of Job* (ET Harold Knight), Nelson 1967.
[2] H. H. Rowley, *Job*, Oliphants 1970.

This book is a search for such answers. The method adopted is thematic. Troubles, it is said, never appear singly.

> 'When sorrows come, they come not single spies,
> But in battalions.'[3]

And it is also true that they rarely have a single aspect. They have physical, intellectual, and spiritual factors. Many such factors are touched on in the Book of Job, though not systematically. What we shall attempt may be compared with the various maps which geographers draw of a country: one to represent rainfall, another population density a third geological structure, and so on.

But simply because this is to be our method, something must be said here and now about Job himself and the book which bears his name.

The origin of the Book of Job is shrouded in mystery. Jewish tradition ascribed it to Moses,[4] but it is thought that the only evidence for this lies in the patriarchal features of the book. Many scholars have dated the work in the post-exilic period on the grounds of its linguistic peculiarities. A sounder argument for late dating of this kind lies in the wealth of allusion to the rest of Old Testament Scripture. Archaeological discovery in the Near East has thrown up a considerable number of works, as we have seen, dealing with justice and human suffering in a way which prove it to have been a traditional theme over hundreds of years. While these show that the Book of Job is a contribution within an agelong discussion, and while there is no need to deny that its writer was familiar with this or comparable literature, it is saying something, as we aim to argue, quite distinctive.

As for the figure of Job himself, he is certainly not a figment of the writer's imagination. The name appears in Ezekiel 14:14, 20 together with the Noah familiar to us from Genesis and (as the New English Bible correctly spells it) a Danel, who is probably not anything to do with the biblical Daniel, but

[3] Shakespeare, *Hamlet*, Act IV, Sc. 5, line 78.
[4] Baba Bathra, 14b.

may well be a king mentioned in literature discovered in the ruins of the Canaanite city of Ras Shamra as one famous for judging fairly and giving protection to widows and orphans. In the last few years, older equivalents of the name Job have turned up in material of the second millennium BC, making it clear that its original meaning was, 'Where is my father?'[5] In view of Job's cry (23:3), 'If only I knew how to find him', it is tempting to imagine that the writer's philology stretched to this explanation! But in any case, Providence chose the right name for the hero of this drama, to say nothing of his being the one who posed most poignantly the question to which Christian access to 'Abba, Father' (Gal. 4:6) is the ultimate answer.

Of course, the very fact that the Book of Job is for the most part in verse is enough to show that the writer treated his theme with some literary freedom. The reference in the Epistle of James (5:11) should warn us against any cavalier dismantling of the factual infrastructure which roots the figure of Job in history. On the other hand, the formula with which the book begins, analogous to the English 'Once upon a time . . .', marks it out as in a different literary category from the historical books of the Old Testament. Moreover, nothing can be so barren as the kind of controversy which still takes place today over the historicity of the book's details. A case is made out later for taking seriously what the book says about Satan, but that case cannot rest on events in the Prologue as though it offered us eye-witness evidence of Satan's activity! On the other hand, to the extent to which the Book of Job is a work of imagination, its 'literary devices' (for those who think this is a good description of Satan) are endorsed by the New Testament as accurate theological mapwork.

Further, if the writer's interest in actual history is in question, it may reasonably be claimed that it was not so much the history of the patriarch Job with which he was concerned as the historical sufferings of the people of Israel. For as the profusion of his references to Isaiah 40–55 makes clear, this is the prism through which light from the story of Job is

[5] M. H. Pope, *Job*, Doubleday 1973, p. 6.

also outside of Israel.

refracted. Or to put the point another way, the story of Job provides an 'Everyman' figure with whom the reader can identify, thus seeing himself within the nation's experience, and learning as an individual the lessons of Israel's history. The Book of Job gathers up the whole of the Old Testament message, and as much as any of its books prepares the way for that mediator between God and man for whom there are such urgent cries within its pages (9 : 32–3, 16 : 21).

By what method are we to relate the message of the Book of Job, written as it was for a cultural setting very different from our own, to our present situation? The first step is to elucidate what the writer was seeking to say to those whom he expected to be its original readers. For this reason, much of what follows is an attempt to spell out his own special interests and emphases. It will be seen that to a greater extent than has often been allowed, the key to this line of exploration lies in the parts of Scripture which were already accepted as authoritative by the writer of Job himself.

Then, secondly, the Book of Job is not only one of the culminating contributions of the Old Testament; it is a part of the whole Bible, including the New Testament. In the light of the New Testament, the book comes to mean something more than, and in some ways different from the sum of its writer's primary intentions. To put the matter in a nutshell, while we see him as providing an answer to certain fundamental human problems, the answer itself is to some extent enigmatic; it poses questions which await further revelation, and that revelation a Christian believes is provided in the events which the New Testament records.

Thirdly, although there is an important element of finality about the biblical revelation, it is not like an obsolete coinage, tied for ever to the time and place in which it is originally current. It is capable of being ever freshly cashed in each succeeding culture and society. Simply to relate the Book of Job to its biblical ancestry in the Old Testament or its biblical issue in the New is not enough to show its relevance to our own day. For we live in an atmosphere created by philosophies peculiar to our own age, and at a time when along with a resurgence of

12

hope that Scripture may hold keys that have been long neglected, there is also a sense of doubt as to whether real and useful bridges can ever be built between the days of its writers and our own.

It needs to be seen clearly that each of the ensuing chapters operates on these three levels of exposition. They are not, however, symmetrical in this respect. In one the demand is for greater emphasis on the writer's intentions, in another on the way in which the New Testament fulfils the teaching of the Book of Job, and in a third on issues which are raised in present-day debate. But this does not alter the main aim, which it is hoped is never lost sight of, namely to show the practical value of the book and its continuing relevance.

The axioms on which this approach is based will be recognized easily enough as the marks of 'conservative theology' —one of the main tenets of which is to take seriously the permit provided by Jesus' own teaching and example to regard the Old Testament as authoritative, and not simply as preparatory scaffolding to be dismantled in the light of fuller revelation. It would not be appropriate to attempt a full defence of this approach. But, on the other hand, it is to be hoped that the analysis of the Book of Job offered here will speak to a circle wider than one consisting only of those who feel they can endorse at the outset such an explicitly high valuation of the Old Testament.

It is not our purpose in the following pages to expound the poem chapter by chapter, as we have explained. So while it is hoped that the theme-studies which lie ahead will drive the reader back to the text, and compel him to become more and more familiar with it, they will be meaningless to one who has not made some prior attempt to acquaint himself with the work as a whole. The following comments on the shape and structure of the Book of Job may prove helpful, particularly in this initial survey.

1 The prologue (Chapters 1 and 2)
Though this, together with the Epilogue, has often been written off as unworthy of the author of the dialogue which forms the

body of the book, it plays a vital part not only in setting the scene for what follows, and hence making the dialogue intelligible, but also in giving the reader an insight into the real reason for Job's sufferings. This lies in God's willingness to allow his own claim to be put to the test—namely, that Job's outstanding service has for its motive something nobler than the self-interest ascribed to Job by Satan.

2 The first cycle of speeches (Chapters 3–14)
The fact that Job complains (Chapter 3) prompts Eliphaz's picture of the holiness of God (Chapters 4–5). The object of Job's complaint (Chapters 6–7) prompt's Bildad's picture of the righteousness of God (Chapter 8). The content of Job's complaint (Chapters 9–10) prompts Zophar's picture of the wisdom of God (Chapter 11).

3 The second cycle of speeches (Chapters 15–21)
The speech by Job at the end of the first cycle (13:23–14:22) leads with its questions about his sins (13:23–28) and his pathetic view of the state of man (14:1–12) into the dominant theme of the second cycle—man and his sin. Here we find (i) Eliphaz speaking of the punishment of sin mainly in terms of the pangs of conscience which attack the wicked (Chapter 15); (ii) Bildad speaking of the hostility which, he says, comes to the ungodly from the whole of nature and particularly other men (Chapter 18); (iii) Zophar concentrating on the bitterness of sin itself once indulged in (Chapter 20).

4 The third cycle of speeches (Chapter 22ff.)
Since Job is completely opposed to their point of view, the final move is for them to do openly what they have so far done only by implication, and charge him point-blank with gross sins. Only Eliphaz and Bildad speak here, and some scholars believe that a third speech for Zophar should be recovered from passages ascribed, as the text stands, to Job.

5 Job's contributions
Though Job answers his friends' arguments, he is more concerned with finding the God who, he thinks, has abandoned him

than with gearing his speeches to the logic of theirs. It is particularly noticeable in the third cycle that he continues his own train of thought as one distracted, and only towards the end comes round to answering his friends' accusations.

6 Elihu's speeches (Chapters 32–37)
Job's three friends are silenced by Job's self-defence, and when he sees this, a young man called Elihu, who has hitherto been listening to the debate unmentioned, intervenes. His anger is kindled equally against Job for making himself out to be righteous, and against the friends for their failure to convince him. They have failed. Yet wisdom is not the perquisite of age, says Elihu, but of God. In this confidence, the young man makes his contribution: or, to be exact, no fewer than four contributions, one after the other.

7 God's intervention and Job's repentance (Chapters 38–42:6)
Job does not make any reply to Elihu, and God who intervenes at this point does not take any notice of him either. Job's plea for an encounter with God is at last answered. But it turns out differently from that which he expects. There is no philosophical answer to the problems that have been discussed. Nor is much notice taken of Job's claim to righteousness, though this is not impugned, and he is commended for realism in the debate with his friends. The burden of the divine contribution is the puny quality of man's formulations when faced with the power and providence of God. In response to this tempestuous onslaught, Job abjectly admits his folly. *Your will.*

8 The epilogue (Chapter 42:7ff.)
After Job has repented, the poem ends with his restoration to the prosperity which was the curtain-raiser for the drama. Restoration indeed is too mild a word. For all Job's assets are carefully doubled. Not, admittedly, his daughters; but daughters scarcely figured in the credit-column of the ancient world. The only conceivable improvement on the original three daughters was that their replacements should be endowed with matchless beauty, and unique power to inherit property.

why not sons. ∴ daughters ok 15

→ daughters not assets.

So afflicted what quality of life + why not curse God + die

unfair. suffering

PART ONE: JOB'S PROBLEM

1 The spiritual enemy

The curtain rises on a picture of integrity and towering greatness. But the reader is allowed only the most fleeting glimpse of the hero and his concern, not only for his own, but also for his children's holiness, before being swept away to the heights of heaven. There a kind of cabinet meeting is in progress, and Job is on the agenda.

When this item of business comes up, we meet Job's spiritual enemy. Has Satan considered, God asks, the matchless character of this outstanding man? With such protection, comes the quick retort, no wonder Job sees fit to behave himself. God is stung by this slur on his relationship with Job, and challenges Satan to test the truth of his insinuation: let Job be stripped of his prosperity.

Satan sets to work with terrible efficiency. A few swift strokes, and family and property are all annihilated. Yet not God's claim: the next meeting comes round, and this is still intact; Job has not abandoned his loyalty, God points out. But neither has Satan abandoned his scepticism. 'Skin for skin!'[1] he says. 'There is nothing a man will grudge to save himself' (2:4). At this, God goes further. This time Satan may attack all but Job's very life. And this is how Job comes to be plagued with his terrible boils. Yet still there is no failure of nerve. It is, ironically, only after Job's friends arrive that he begins to complain.

Satan's part in the plot is thus quickly told. But who is this

[1] Many suggestions have been put forward to explain this dictum. The most attractive answer is one which N. H. Tur-Sinai puts forward only to reject it—namely, that the words are glossed in the text immediately afterwards: 'All that a man has he will give for his life.' If so, the meaning will be, 'One skin *a man will give up* for another'. The objection to this, says Tur-Sinai, is that 'barter does not involve the exchange of one thing for another of the same kind'. But the truth of this observation may well give the proverb its punch: 'One (kind of) skin—i.e. property, valued in animal-hides—a man will give up for another—i.e. his own skin'.

Satan? The modern reader has some questions in his mind before he can see his way to grasping the spiritual relevance of a book beginning with such a strange cartoon.

1 Is Satan in the book of Job the same Satan as appears in the New Testament?

Some doubt has been cast on the answer to this question by the fact that in the Hebrew text of Job, we find '*the* Satan'. That is, the phrase is not grammatically a proper name. It is as though the word designated some office, and comparison with Zechariah 3:1 suggests some such equivalent as 'public prosecutor'. Tur-Sinai has suggested that the figure and role of Satan derived from the Persian secret service, whose officers, according to Herodotus, were called the 'eyes and ears of the king'. But this brings us face to face with the major difficulty. Is Satan then a minister in the divine cabinet? This is scarcely consistent with the New Testament picture, we might think, where (to persevere with parliamentary language) Satan is clearly the leader of the opposition rather than a member of the government.

Let us then examine the problem more deeply. The first point to notice is that there is some evidence in Job that Satan is the *servant* of God. He appears, as we have noticed, along with other 'sons of God' at the meeting of the celestial council. 'Sons of God' in this context (they are called 'angels' in the Septuagint) are simply superhuman or heavenly beings, in contrast to ordinary mortals or 'sons of men'. But perhaps Satan is there as an observer, or even gate-crashing. This, however, does not fit in with God's summons to render account of his activity. 'Going to and fro on the earth' (1:7 RSV), we must understand, is not a confession of diabolic idleness; it is rather a claim that he has been doing his duty zealously as a criminal investigator. Further, we notice that Satan is far from being a free agent. He takes orders from God, and he cannot go an inch beyond the length of rope allowed him by his master. His appearance for interview, his accountability, and this bondage to divine commands add up to a portrait of one who is unquestionably a servant of God.

On the other hand, we find equally convincing evidence that Satan is the *enemy* of God. First, he is cynical about the truth of God's statements. God declares that Job is a man of outstanding character. Satan's answer amounts to saying that Job is not a man of outstanding character at all: simply one who knows which side his bread is buttered. Bad enough to call God a liar in anybody else's hearing: Satan does not hesitate to do so to his face. Bad enough to indulge in calumny on the basis of evidence: Satan's insinuations are supported by no evidence at all, and his failure to observe the elements of deuteronomic law-court procedure (which required more than one witness to substantiate any indictment) would not have been lost on the original readers (Deuteronomy 19:15).

Moreover, Satan is cynical not only about God's assessment, but also about Job's profession. Satan is hostile to God in his dealings *tête à tête* with him, but it is reflected too in malevolence towards God's choicest men. God is a liar: his servant is a hypocrite. When Satan suggests that Job should be tested by stripping him of the outward marks of God's favour, we see the same motive that led Joseph's brothers to strip him of the coat which symbolized his father's special love: jealousy. And when all this fails to produce the breach in Job's loyalty to God which Satan promises, we see the bud of jealousy ripen in cruelty: Job is consigned to the rubbish-dump outside the city to scratch his sores.

Satan, therefore, is both the servant and the enemy of God. When Davidson says[2] that Satan is the opposer of men *because* he is the minister of God, he coins a phrase which, while in a sense defensible, is liable to be misleading. For it suggests that in the Book of Job Satan is related to God as the Gestapo was to Hitler, as though he were neither more nor less than a tool in the divine hand.

Now if this were in fact the case, it would mean a flat contradiction between the theological presentation of the Book of Job and what we find, for example, in the Epistle of James. There (1:13) it is insisted that temptation does not come from God,

---

[2] A. B. Davidson, *The Book of Job* (Cambridge Bible for Schools and Colleges, 1903), p. xxxii.

though this is, of course, balanced by the earlier precept, 'Whenever you have to face trials of many kinds, count yourselves supremely happy in the knowledge that such testing of your faith breeds fortitude' (1 : 2, 3). But this balance between God's allowing believers to be tested, and yet not being directly responsible for the testing, is precisely the balance which, however picturesquely, the Book of Job presents. It is true that James in these passages does not refer in so many words to Satan. But the same basic pattern is found in Matthew's Gospel, where we read (4 : 1), 'Jesus was led away *by the Spirit* into the wilderness to be tempted *by the devil'*. Indeed we find this outlook reflected in the words of Jesus himself at a place no less familiar than the Lord's Prayer: 'Lead us not into temptation'. These New Testament passages represent the same basic position as the Book of Job. There likewise we find God's express permission for Job to be tempted; but equally, we find God expressly dissociated from the temptation. Unless both these things are said, no justice is done to the writer's approach.

2 Does the Bible teach a unitary and consistent doctrine of Satan throughout?

To take the matter a stage further, it is often said that there are many different theologies in the Bible. And in supposed accordance with this view, the variety of treatments accorded to Satan and the problem of evil is seen as evidence for the belief that Scripture speaks with many voices. Therefore we must ask ourselves the question, 'Is there any development of the idea of Satan to be traced in the Bible?'

The answer is twofold. To begin with, there is definitely a development in *expression*. Take first of all the statement in 2 Samuel 24 : 1 that 'the Israelites felt the Lord's anger when he incited David against them'.[3] This is reproduced by the Chronicler, one of the later writers of the Old Testament, as

[3] The NEB follows the traditional interpretation of the verse. But it is perhaps worth considering the possibility that the correct translation should be, 'when David was incited'. For the indefinite use of the third person singular (similar to German 'man', French 'on') see Gesenius, *Hebrew Grammar*, ed. and enl. E. Kautzsch, 2nd English edition, tr. A. E. Cowley, Clarendon 1910, para. 144d.

follows: '*Satan*, setting himself against Israel, incited David to count the people'. Here we find no definite article: 'Satan' is a proper name, as everywhere in the New Testament.

Between these two passages, we may notice two others. The first is in 1 Kings 22:19–23, where again we find the same kind of divine cabinet as in the Prologue of Job. Here there is an unnamed evil spirit, but one whose role is not unlike that of the figure in Job. The second passage is even more similar. In Zechariah 3, the definite article is used—'*the* Satan'—even where Satan is addressed (3:2), and the rebuke administered there by the angel of God is comparable with the way in which Satan is taken to task in Job.

It is likely that the Job passage is dependent on the one in Zechariah. But in any case, we can discern four stages of development, as follows: (i) incitement to evil ascribed to God or to an indefinite third person (2 Sam. 24:1, cf. 1 Sam. 26:19); (ii) an evil spirit, though unnamed, is found in the divine council (I Kings 22:19–23); (iii) this evil spirit referred to as '*the* Satan' (Zech. 3, Job 1–2); (iv) the article dropped, and 'Satan' used now as a proper name, as in the New Testament (I Chr. 21:1).

Does this developing use of language represent four different theologies? No doubt the word 'theology' could be defined in such a way as to make the answer 'yes'. But against the theory that the Bible speaks with a babel of conflicting voices, an alternative view can be illustrated by an analogy from photography.

We can take a black and white snap of an object and compare it first with one taken on colour film, and then with one which is three-dimensional. The photographs will all be different, but they may all be accurate representations within the limits of the technique adopted. It is arguable that something of the same sort explains the developing theology of the Bible.

If this is so, it is important to see that when the writer of Chronicles introduced Satan into his version of the story in 2 Samuel 24, he was not contradicting the earlier writer, but rather guarding the earlier literature against misunderstanding at a later stage. Precisely the same point can be made from the

Book of Job itself. In the Prologue, we find Job's misfortunes ascribed to Satan. In the Epilogue, on the other hand, they are ascribed to God: 'all the evil that the Lord had brought upon him' (43:11). L. W. Batten, seeing here an intolerable conflict, says that this 'ignores and probably excludes the Satan stories of the Prologue'.[4] On the contrary, what it shows is that the writer of the Book of Job, though prepared to take over the figure of Satan—as we have seen, he may not have been the first to do so—does not thereby adopt the dualism characteristic of the Persian religion from which the figure of Satan derived. He wants, on the contrary, to assert that God is indeed *in a sense* responsible for, or at least in sovereign control over, Satan's activity.

3 What is the importance of Satan in the Book of Job?
The Prologue has often been regarded as a trivial and unworthy introduction to what is universally regarded as a great poem. And it is probable that the presence of the figure of Satan has contributed to this conclusion. But there are two crucial reasons why any such approach to the Book of Job is to be resisted, and why the Prologue should be seen as an indispensable element in the work as a whole.

First, the presence of Satan is vital for the reader to judge the deficiency of the arguments and conclusions of Job's friends. They imagine that God is punishing Job. The reader knows from the outset that the position is completely different. Far from arising out of God's anger with him, his sufferings are actually the result of God's utmost approval of him.

Further, not only are the friends wrong in their conclusion about God's attitude to Job; they are wrong too in the unsympathetic view which they adopt to what Job himself says. They regard his language as completely inexcusable. But the reader knows that it has been diabolically provoked, that it is the desperate response of one who has been put through the sternest conceivable test.

The second thing is this. The figure of Satan is important because it enables the writer to sketch out a doctrine which

---

[4] *American Theological Review*, xv (1933), p. 127.

avoids the errors of dualism and of its opposite, 'monism'. Dualism means that view of the world according to which the spiritual forces of good and evil are independent of each other, and this often means that the issue between them is in ultimate doubt. Monism, on the other hand, sees the whole of nature as an integrated organism, so that all that is is a manifestation of God. The most famous historical example of such a view is that of the Dutch philosopher, Spinoza, and his work illustrates the weakness of any monistic view, which lies in its failure to deal adequately with the problem of evil, since evil has to be regarded as unreal.

Far from marking out the writer as simple-minded or primitive, the figure of Satan in the Book of Job enables him to pioneer an advance in the biblical understanding of good and evil which is not only highly sophisticated, but has in principle never been improved upon. Nor is this a matter of merely academic interest; it strikes at the heart, as we shall see, of issues which are very much alive today both in the realm of thought and in that of practical Christian living.

4 What is to be learned today from the treatment of Satan in Job?

The words 'monism' and 'dualism' may be unfamiliar, but the patterns of thought which they label are very prevalent. Think first of those who regard everything as having a 'scientific explanation'. For such people, everything that exists is part of one enormous machine, and besides this machine there is nothing. To every question there is either a mechanistic answer (that is, one in terms of cause and effect), or there is no answer at all. But when the scientific method over-reaches itself in such an extreme way, the concepts of good and evil lose their meaning. For example, it is not appropriate on such a view for anybody to be praised or blamed, for the individual is only a focus of events for which he is not in any real sense responsible. In practice this philosophy is difficult to apply in any thoroughgoing way. For what parent goes through life imputing his children's naughtiness either to their genes or their environment? But this simply draws attention to the fundamental shortcomings of the theory. The Christian insists that moral choices are real. And this is understood in terms of pleasing or failing to please a personal God. But it is precisely in the possibility of failing to please that the monist's problem arises. Why should anyone fail to please an almighty, creator God? The doctrine of Satan may leave some questions unanswered; but at least it answers this one.

However, the barrenness of scientific monism is driving more and more people today into an equal and opposite error. On the one hand, there are those who consult the stars. For them, good and evil are like the two sides of a coin which is tossed. But any view which makes evil autonomous is dualistic. And, one may add, pessimistic. The important feature of the account given in the Book of Job, which is, as we have seen, in its essentials the characteristic developed position of Scripture, is that it depicts an evil spirit whose power is real, but limited.

Both monism and dualism have crucial weaknesses, which may be summarized as follows: the monist cannot answer the question how evil exists at all; the dualist cannot explain, if evil is supposed to be an independent force, the evidence for God's unquestionable power. Evil is a terrible thing, but even pagan philosophers have been prepared to admit that at its worst it is but a stain on God's many-splendoured world. The biblical view marches between the horns of the dilemma.

But can we take seriously the existence of such an evil spirit as we find portrayed in the Bible? Anyone who advocates doing so is conscious of the difficulties which such an idea presents to the mind of modern man, and we need to grapple with the reasons for such misgivings.

(i) In the first place, it is felt that any serious talk of a devil belongs to the thought world of a former generation. Horns and forked tail fix him in a Christendom which has passed away. And preparedness to sacrifice the horns and forked tail in the interests of modernization does not go far enough to satisfy those who are sceptical. The feeling is that all biblical language about such a spiritual enemy has to be radically re-translated—or to use the more accurate, technical word, 'demythologized'. 'We explain things differently today' means that just as we no longer view the world through Hebrew spectacles as something supported on pillars beneath a solid heaven, so we speak about evil in psychological language which avoids any reference to devils.

(ii) Thus, secondly, there is the feeling that we are never in a position to put our finger on Satan's activity. Alternative explanations are always available. An earthquake can be explained in terms of geological fault-lines, schizophrenia in terms of psychology or environment or even chemistry.

(iii) Finally, the problem of accounting for the origin of Satan is thought to outweigh the advantages of positing his existence. Did God make Satan? The Bible scarcely says so. And the difficulty of filling in such details argues against ascribing to him real-life existence. Further, there is not, as has been admitted, an entirely uniform picture of Satan in the Bible. If one were to admit his existence, would it be the Satan of the Book of Job, or the Satan of I Peter, or what?

The place of Satan in the Book of Job cannot be written off as secondary or trivial. Therefore it is imperative to answer these questions if we are to make any estimate of the relevance of the work to the present day. Let us look then at these three areas of objection in turn.

(i) Some reply has already been given to the question of the 'cash value' of the mythological language used to describe Satan in Scripture in the discussion above of monism and dualism. To resort to a world-view which does without such a figure, one is driven into a Spinoza-like philosophy which cannot present any adequate account of evil: either it has to be explained away in terms of absence of good (which fails to represent the malicious element that our experience so often illustrates) or it has to be ascribed directly to God himself, which, if not unthinkable, raises much more mountainous philosophical problems.

Another way of putting this point is to say that if the process of demythologizing is carried to the lengths of evicting the devil altogether, one has done something different from translating the thought of the Bible into modern idiom. The whole presentation of God's dealings with man is distorted at a most crucial point, thus moving the question out of the area of 'How shall we understand what the Bible is saying?' into the area of 'Can we accept what the Bible is saying at all?'

(ii) The second area of objection is one which introduces us to well-trodden ground in modern philosophy. One is straightaway reminded of the parable by which John Wisdom[5] likened God to a gardener who was never seen and never heard. What is the value of such a hypothesis, he asked, and why should we not be content with merely describing the phenomena, instead of importing a figure about whom one knew no more than the phenomena themselves disclosed? Wisdom used this argument, of course, to urge the uselessness of belief in God. But here it may serve us differently. If the argument is valid, then it is valid against any form of theism. If the argument is invalid, then it is just as invalid to destroy the case for believing in Satan as it is to destroy the case for believing in God. In other words, any attempt to displace Satan by alternative explanations either proves too little or too much.

The biblical concept of causation constantly demands two levels of explanation. The Jews are brought home from Babylon by the edict of Cyrus, but also by the mercy of God. When Peter demurred at the suggestion of Jesus's death, Jesus saw in what he said not merely the word of man, but the word of Satan. And again we must insist that reducing this two-level scheme to one level to comply with modern thought is not interpretation, but distortion of the biblical idiom. For ultimately what is being demanded is that all the contents of the Bible's spiritual categories should be rehoused in the categories of this world: a project which has to be pronounced less promising than putting new wine into old wineskins.

[5] First published in the *Proceedings of the Aristotelian Society*, 1944–5; reprinted as ch. X in *Logic and Language*, Vol. I (1951) and in *Philosophy and Psychoanalysis* (1953). See also A. G. N. Flew and Alasdair MacIntyre (eds.) *New Essays in Philosophical Theology*, SCM 1955, p. 96.

(iii) Finally, it has to be admitted that the Bible does not supply us with answers to many of the questions which can be raised about Satan. His origin is shrouded in obscurity (as, of course, also is the question, 'Who made God?'). But the fact that the biblical account of Satan is not exhaustive is no reason for regarding it as inadequate as far as it goes. And it is not wholly unfair to fill out Satan's role in the Book of Job by reference to the New Testament. For first, it is possible to exaggerate the difference between the two pictures, ignoring the fact that one is the literary ancestor of the other. And second, one must resist the tendency to play down the extent to which earlier writings in the canon of Scripture came to have a developed meaning in the light of later revelation.

But granting that there is a variety of mythological language from very diverse sources, we have no need to admit that there is in reality nothing to which the picture language actually refers, any more than we need give up a belief in the existence of Cleopatra when we find her referred to by Shakespeare in one place as Egypt and in another as a serpent.

No apology needs to be made for wrestling with this issue at the intellectual level. For it is at an intellectual level that Satan delights to make himself *incognito*, and those who deny his existence do so for what they fancy to be intellectual reasons. Nevertheless, it is in the practical realm where the proceeds of one belief and another are cashed, and to this we must now turn.

When we do so, there are two points of view which we may adopt: that of Job, and that of Job's friends.

It is, as we have argued earlier, an important feature of the Book of Job that the reader knows what Job does not know. It is precisely because Job cannot proceed beyond the assumption that God is doing this to him that some of his most serious misgivings arise. Of course, there is another question, even when Satan's part in the plot is allowed for—namely, why God allows Satan to do this to Job. As we shall see, the writer answers this question at the end of the book in a way which complements what he teaches at the outset. But he wants his readers to learn something from their privileged glimpse of the celestial cabinet which will be of use when they have to stand in Job's shoes or something like them. When the believer suffers, it is not through any failure of love or oversight on the part of God. It is because of the jealousy of his spiritual enemy.

And there is a subtler point to notice. Satan achieved nothing by his direct onslaught, either at stage one or at stage two. Job can still say, 'If we accept good from God, shall we not accept evil?' (2:10). But what he could not do by frontal assault, he could at least begin to do under cover of Job's friends. Satan's cynical conviction was that nobody would serve God except for the resulting material prosperity. And in Job's friends, he found allies in this conviction. Their ill-concealed accusations that Job's sufferings were a form of divine punishment provided Satan with a much sharper weapon than any he had used in the Prologue. Jesus once rebuked one of his closest friends for adopting the role of Satan (Matt. 16:23); and whether the bullets arrive in the shape of bad advice or cold comfort, the believer can learn here to be on his guard against the possibility that his spiritual enemy may start firing at him from the most unexpected positions.

In the Epistle to the Ephesians, Paul provides the Christian with a complete suit of armour (Eph. 6:11 ff.). But one prerequisite for using armour either for defence or attack is recognition of the enemy. This is why the important reminder is included that our fight is not against human foes, but 'against cosmic powers, against the authorities and potentates of this dark world, against the superhuman forces of evil in the heavens'. All this frightening description is synonymous with 'the devil', against whose devices the Apostle is urging his readers to stand firm. The Book of Job is likewise an urgent summons for those under attack to recognize their true enemy.

But he also needs to be recognized when he seeks to treat us like Job's friends. In their case the enemy managed to pull the wool over their eyes in two ways. In the first place, they failed to recognize the part that he was playing in Job's troubles before ever they arrived on the scene. But much more sinister than this, they failed to recognize the way in which the enemy was actually using them to destroy one whom they thought of as their friend. However, in touching on the faults of Job's friends, we are trespassing on a subject too important to be dismissed in a paragraph: they must have a chapter to themselves at a later stage.

2 Serious illness and the threat of death

The last enemy, as the Apostle Paul dubbed death, is for today's society the last obscenity. Nakedness in any other quarter is acceptable, and a variety of matters which were taboo a generation ago can be freely discussed. But death is shrouded in a thick veil. Doctors tend not to mention it: it is the one thing which the patient must never consider. And even after death has taken place, its implications are evaded by those who have their dead loved ones made up to look living, while some even talk seriously about the deep-freezing of corpses till a remedy for death is discovered. The same atmosphere surrounds serious disease. As with death, so with cancer—it is a forbidden word. No wonder that the medical profession is deeply disturbed about the wisdom of all this, for it has to be admitted that the present philosophy is rooted in dishonesty.

Man's last enemy is not made less frightening by attempts to disguise it. If anything, the reverse is the case: death becomes even more fearful for many because of the general refusal to face its reality. However, the Book of Job tears off the veil. Part of the enduring value of the work lies in the way disease and death are here squarely faced, and our purpose in this chapter is first of all to unravel what is said about these things, and then to assess its significance for a Christian understanding.

We meet Job first in the light of a dazzling sunset. And at the end he is transfigured by a glorious new dawn. But between the curtain-raiser and the Epilogue the long night is haunted by the death which Job schizophrenically both desires and shuns. Death is also the subject of a raging controversy between the one who stood on its threshold and those who were supposed to be his comforters. Nowhere else in Scripture are we at such close quarters with man's ultimate destiny. Nor is there anywhere more material for coming to grips with the biblical understanding of death.

Job's view of death is far from self-consistent. But there is value in studying it because he both mirrors the hopes and fears of the natural man, and also in important ways points us in the direction of Christian faith. Our approach will be to examine three salient characteristics of death in order to clarify the different phases of Job's experience.

1 The restfulness of death

What Job's disease was is much disputed. Some think that it was elephantiasis. They argue that the strangling sensation (Job 7:15, 30:18), the nightmarish dreams (7:14), profuse weeping (16:16), disfigurement (2:12), and the peeling of blackened skin (30:30) are all symptoms of this disease. On the other hand, the onset of pain seems to have been sudden. And other symptoms, such as maggot-ridden ulcers (7:5), fetid breath (19:17) and emaciation (19:20) add to the impression that more than one disease is being described. Job is an every-man figure and there is a sense in which all our symptoms converge in him. It is an important point that whatever illnesses a reader may bring to this book they will never add up to a greater burden than Job's.

However, if this factor was in the writer's mind, it is another which seems to have been uppermost. This is the connection between his description of Job and the diseases described in Deuteronomy 28. In verses 27 and 35 of that chapter, two distinct ailments, though each affecting the skin, are mentioned. And Job seems to have symptoms of both. If so, the reader is evidently intended to conclude that precisely those terrors threatened by Deuteronomy for disobedience to God are here found afflicting one who is noted for his obedience.

At any rate, Job is here found physically *in extremis*: a week's protracted silence on the part of his friends had done nothing to relieve his agony. No wonder then that the poetic dialogue begins with an outburst in which Job professes a longing for what he conceives of as the release of death. 'Why was I born at all?' he complains (Job 3:1–10). 'Why, if I had to be born alive, could I not have been exposed?' (3:12–16). Then he would have been at rest, lying in the quiet grave, asleep in death (3:13). Throughout the remainder of this speech of his, the idea is reiterated. Rich and poor, the tyrant and the man who has worked so slavishly for him share the same repose in death, and in death the prisoner of war finds peace (3:18). Why could Job not find that rest, that peace? Instead, he says,

> Every terror that haunted me has caught up with me,
> and all that I feared has come upon me.
> There is no peace of mind not quiet for me;
> I chafe in torment and have no rest (3:25–26).

A third millennium Egyptian text[1] shows us that suicide was not unknown in the Ancient East. So it is pertinent to notice in passing that in this chapter suicide is not even mentioned as a possibility—let alone euthanasia.

There is a story that Bishop Taylor Smith was once asked in a train what he made of the theory that after death there is just nothing. 'Very optimistic', came the reply. No doubt the bishop pursued the conversation further from this point. But his answer, as it stands *tout court*, epitomizes the response of Job's friends to his professed longing for death. Job had said,

> If a man dies, can he live again?
> He shall never be roused from his sleep.
> If only thou wouldst hide me in Sheol ... (14:12–13).

In their context, these words express despair rather than hope. But Job is falling back on the thought that even if there is no waking beyond the grave, at least there is sleep. But, if Dhorme's reconstruction is correct, Bildad harbours the words against him, and, with a cruel twist to Psalm 139:8, he says later,

> In the underworld the shades writhe in fear,
> the waters and all that live in them are struck with terror.
> Sheol is laid bare,
> and Abaddon uncovered before him (26:5–6).

[1] J. B. Pritchard (ed.), *Ancient Near Eastern Texts relating to the Old Testament*, Princeton University Press (3rd edition 1969), pp. 405 ff.

Thus Job is warned not to imagine that in death there will be any getting away from God—or any peace.

Of course, Bildad, by this stage if not at the outset, had come to the conclusion that Job was anything but a godly man, and the traditional viewpoint which he upheld did allow that the righteous found rest in death. Thus Eliphaz portrays good men coming to their graves in serenity, like sheaves at harvest-time to the threshing floor, their offspring thick as grass upon the earth (5:25–26). This last phrase is very important, because it gives the clue to what was considered the source of peace in the good man's death: his children were an extension of his personality; their existence transformed death from something utterly tragic into something at least tolerable.

But Job rejects the idyllic portrait painted by Eliphaz of what happens to the righteous, though he does point out that such serenity often characterizes the death of the wicked (21:13). However, this brings us up against a thorough-going inconsistency in Job's outlook. For while, as we have seen, he at various points longs for death as something which will bring him rest, this idea is a somewhat self-conscious overlay. Beneath it there keeps appearing a deep-seated horror of death, which we must now examine.

2 The fearfulness of death
One recurring theme which expresses very vividly the frightening character of death is its constant association with darkness. It is a place of shadow and gloom (3:5, 10:21–2), which makes natural the comparison with the womb (10:19, cf. 1:21). The word 'darkness' is enough to signify death (15:22, 18:18, 20:26). Life is like the working day of the casual labourer, and death is the setting of his unhappy sun (7:2).[2]

In order to understand this association between death and darkness more clearly, one must rid oneself of a hangover from the classical Graeco-Roman tradition about the underworld. Dhorme is probably right in explaining the imagery found in Job (and elsewhere in the Old Testament) by the nature of Phoenician tombs. These were underground cavities, and the

[2] Dhorme, op. cit., p. 98.

entrance was a narrow vertical tunnel. Hence the expression 'pit', which is a synonym commonly found in Job (17:14 lit., 33:18, 22), and in the Psalms, for death. Hence also the idea of a tunnel down which the dead pass. This is probably mistranslated in the New English Bible as 'river of death' (33:18, 36:12) and 'pit' (33:28). It is easy to see, therefore, how the Phoenician type of tomb accentuated the quality of darkness associated with death, though the fact that the dead no longer 'see the light' makes this a natural image and one which is found universally. What concerns us here, however, is that what is dark is unknown and therefore fearful.

Another feature linked to that of the darkness of the pit is the conception of death as a prison. In 17:16, Job speaks of the 'bars' of Sheol (RV). There is no need to adopt the NEB emendation in view of the mention, in the mouth of God (38:17), of the 'gates' of Sheol, a very similar idea. Elsewhere, Death is referred to (by Bildad at 18:14) as the king of terrors, in a passage which depicts Death as an ogre with a dungeon full of victims.

Death is fearful too because of its inevitability and because of the shortness of life. Thus, though Job complains that his own life is dragging on too long, he can also with a certain sick humour refer to death as the arrival of the serviceman's relief, or the end of the navvy's working day (7:1-2, 6-7). All through his term of service, the soldier dreams of what he will do when he 'gets outside'. But demobilization for man is no sweet evening of release, but the end. All day long the labourer works for his pay, but man's sunset wage-packet is simply his tomb.

Another graphic image makes life a wisp of straw blown by the wind or a fragment of chaff in a tornado. With devastating swiftness we are hustled away. Like the imperial despatch-rider our days flash by (9:25). Without warning the shuttle-thread gives out (7:6). The moments of life go past as swiftly as the reed-built skiffs which carried the Nubian ambassadors down the Nile to Egypt (Isa. 18:2, Job 9:26) or (less playfully) like vultures swooping on carrion. Man's hope is swept away like stones in a landslide, or soil after heavy rain (14:18-19).

3 The finality of death

Much of the imagery which we have been looking at carries
with it the implication of finality. The stone which falls down
the mountain never returns to its place. The river flows only
in one direction. The blown chaff is never seen again. But Job
also dwells quite explicitly on the finality of death (7:9–10,
10:21–22).

Yet there is at this point the crucial inconsistency in Job's
attitude which is mentioned above. Does he not, it may be
asked, express the hope of resurrection? This poses one of the
most controversial questions faced by interpreters of the book.

Two passages deserve consideration in connection with this
problem. The first is 14:13–14:

> If only thou wouldst hide me in Sheol
> and conceal me till thy anger turns aside,
> if thou wouldst fix a limit for my time there, and then remember
> me!
> Then I would not lose hope, however long my service,
> waiting for my relief to come.

If Sheol were, like earthly life, a period of service to which
God set a term, if only there were a time when one's relief
could be expected to come and release one from one's tour of
duty, then certainly this would provide some answer to Job's
problem. But close attention to the context makes it clear that
this fantasy is but wishful thinking. There is hope for a tree,
if it be cut down, that its stump will spring to life again (14:7).
But man dies and remains lifeless (v. 10), never to rise till the
very sky splits open. This last phrase provides food for Christian thought: but on Job's lips, to wait for the sky to split
open is to wait for ever.

The second passage, on the other hand (19:23 ff.), marks a
considerable step forward towards Christian hope. Sadly, the
verses concerned have notorious textual uncertainties. But it is
beyond dispute that they express the hope of future vindication.
The question is simply whether this vindication is something
which Job expects to see in earthly life or beyond. In the light

of the pessimism which is characteristic, as we have just seen, of Job's attitude to death, the former alternative might seem the more obvious. And it is vindication in this life which he in fact experiences at last. But verses 23–24 prohibit this interpretation:

> O that my words might be inscribed,
> O that they might be engraved in an inscription,
> cut with an iron tool and filled with lead
> to be a witness in hard rock!

The whole point here, whatever the exact translation might be, is that Job wants his apologia to outlast his lifetime. It follows that what is described in the succeeding verses (25–27) refers to an experience beyond death.

However, if this interpretation is correct, we are left with a contradiction: Job both discounts anything beyond the grave (in many of the passages we have looked at), and then affirms it (in this one). But this contradiction is not so stark as at first appears. Certainly the hope of resurrection is expressed—or something like it. But it is expressed as a hope against hope; as the logical consequence of faith in a God who must somehow, sometime, satisfy the claims of justice relating to one for whom death is imminent and inevitable.

What we are left with, therefore, is a tension in Job's mind between his refusal at bottom to abandon his belief in a righteous God, and on the other hand his experience that Sheol is a place of no return. This tension is never wholly resolved within the book, and any solution must take account of the fact that the final chapters in a sense retreat from resurrection faith to the idyll of earthly restoration. The writer of the book, we must conclude, has Job expressing (if wistfully) the hope of resurrection, but it can scarcely be claimed that he gives it unreserved endorsement. What we have here may perhaps be likened to a preliminary drawing-board sketch of a building which still lies from a human point of view almost entirely in the realm of fantasy.

4 The Christian perspective

When we view the Book of Job, however, in the light of the New Testament account of death and resurrection, the Job who was, even for his own biographer, the dreamer of somewhat insubstantial dreams, or maybe the tentative pioneer of a new approach to death, becomes a prophet raising the curtain on the Christian revelation.

In his despair, Job speaks the truth by happy irony, and quite unwittingly. The skies he thought of as certain to remain forever unbroken have in one sense already parted for Christ to come and will in a much more radical sense open when he returns to call the buried from their tombs (Mark 14:62, I Thess. 4:16).

And in his forlorn hope, with the wildness of a drowning man clutching at straws, he puts into words what in the New Testament is transformed from the tiny ray which pierces Job's bleak darkness into the full-orbed glory of resurrection light. The early Christians, thrown to lions, ignited as torches (though innocent of all charges) at Nero's festivities, died in the conviction, much less wavering than Job's, that their redeemer lives and will one day appear to vindicate them.

There is here, admittedly, an intuitive jump. 'I know that my redeemer lives' are words which have been immortalized by their use in Handel's *Messiah* and in the funeral service. But what are we to say of this kind of borrowing? Does the source of the quotation play a part in its meaning on Christian lips? If so, can the transfer be regarded as theologically legitimate? Or is it faulted by the criticism that it involves an old-fashioned view of Scripture which fails to take account of changes in context and theological presuppositions from one part to another? It is with such questions in mind that we conclude by spelling out the ways in which a Christian may learn from the Book of Job in his consideration of death and serious illness.

The Old Testament has evidential value for Christian faith wherever it anticipates the New Testament's message. The references to resurrection in the Book of Job fit into a great network of passages which, taken together, provide a cumulative foundation for the Christian doctrine. These passages are of three kinds, which must now be briefly distinguished from one another.

(i) In the first place, there are a large number of accounts in the Old Testament of what we may call earthly restoration after the kind of crises which, while not involving death itself, contain the gravest threat of it. Into this category come such incidents as the survival of Noah, the sparing of Isaac, the elevation of Joseph, Israel's safe crossing of the Red Sea, the emergence of outlawed David from the murderous hands of Saul, Daniel's escape from the den of lions and that of the three children from the burning fiery furnace. These passages foreshadow the New Testament doctrine of resurrection in the same kind of way that the births of Isaac, Samson, Samuel and John the Baptist—all with mothers who had long been barren —presage the miraculous birth of Jesus. The humanly impossible paves the way for the humanly even more impossible. Some of the passages we have mentioned were already seen in an analogous way by later writers in the Old Testament itself as preparing for the crowning Old Testament miracle—the return from exile. Indeed this particular earthly restoration, together with the rebuilding of the Jerusalem Temple, constitutes the preparation *par excellence* for the resurrection of Christ.

(ii) But there are also two kinds of passages in which the idea of resurrection is explicitly mentioned. First there are those which make use of it *figuratively*. Thus the phrase in Hosea 6:2 RSV,

After two days he will revive us;
On the third day he will raise us up

refers primarily to Israel's restoration from captivity. The same kind of explanation applies to Ezekiel's graphic description of the valley of dry bones coming to life again (ch. 37), and perhaps to the Psalmist's conviction that he would at last find glory (Psa. 73:24), where the translation is disputed, but earthly restoration may be in the writer's mind.

(iii) Then finally there are other passages where the idea of resurrection is clearly present without the possibility of any figurative interpretation. Most obvious here are the stories of actual resurrections associated with Elijah and Elisha (I Kgs. 17:22, II Kgs. 4:35). And there are two other passages where it is disputed whether or not they should be understood figuratively rather than literally, but with the balance arguably lying in favour of the latter. One is Psalm 49:15 RSV,

> But God will ransom my soul from the power of Sheol,
> for he will receive me.

The other is Isa. 53:10. Here whatever allowances may be made for the view that the servant who is suffering is the purified people of Israel, there can be no doubt that what is actually described is an individual sufferer, and one who is rescued after (rather than at the point of) death:

> Yet the Lord took thought for his tortured servant
> and healed him who had made himself a sacrifice for sin.

There is a sense in which the Book of Job offers us material to go under all three of these headings. There is in the first place the remarkable reversal of a seemingly hopeless situation, when Job is restored to his former prosperity. There is at any rate one passage, as we have seen, which hazards the idea of actual resurrection. And then we might say that because Job's faith was greeted by earthly restoration, the book as a whole has close affinities with the second category of passages outlined above, where the idea of resurrection is used figuratively.

Now when a Christian looks at this scriptural material and the place which the Book of Job occupies within it, the claim that Jesus rose from the dead is given a context which altogether transforms its character. Without the Old Testament, it might seem reasonable to dismiss the resurrection as a highly unlikely figment of somebody's imagination. But when it is seen as the crowning stone of a pyramid of scriptural under-girding, it becomes not only more meaningful but more credible. The Old Testament not only interprets, but corroborates what the New Testament teaches.

It was to Jews, to those who might have been expected to have searched the Scriptures that Paul addressed the question, 'Why is it considered incredible among you that God should raise dead men to life?' Indeed he says quite plainly that it is in the light of promises made to their forefathers that the preaching of the resurrection deserves credence. Similarly, the risen Jesus, faced with incredulity, lays strong and repeated emphasis on the testimony of the Old Testament (Luke 24:25 ff.).

For a Christian to recover the message of the Old Testament is to re-enter an inheritance which has been there from the beginning, but one which has lately become more and more neglected—with the precise result that the doctrine of the resurrection is under heavy fire in the Church today. The Book of Job is a corner of the garden which may require more hoeing than other parts to bear its appointed fruit, but it is no exaggeration to claim that it gathers together and epitomizes in its pages much of the Old Testament's preparation for the rising of Christ from the dead.

However, if those Christians who down the years have drawn rich comfort from the Book of Job were asked the question, 'How did it help you?', not all would answer with the verse, 'I know that my redeemer lives'. Many would think first of the trials which they had faced, the agony of pain, the squalor of disease, the inability to sleep, the despair of recovery, and the way in which they had found these symptoms mirrored in the Book of Job. To borrow famous words used to describe Ezekiel, Job had sat where they sat. Here there was no attempt to brush the patient's complaint aside, no pretence that there was 'nothing serious'. In Job the reader feels that the realities of human life are faced in all their starkness with utter honesty.

And Job was no crook. That insistent question, 'Why is it happening to me?' finds its quiet rejoinder in another: 'Why was it happening to him?' Simply the picture of a godly man going through the same hard experiences as oneself removes the terrible loneliness which is sometimes the most grievous sting of severe suffering.

Of course, this would be cold comfort if we did not find that for Job there was a way through. The reason why a Christian can face the harsh facts squarely and look into the face of death in this way is because he knows there is a remedy. There is hope, a way of escape from seemingly so secure a jail. Yet it is salutary for him to see the harsh reality. It reminds him of the price at which his escape has been purchased by Jesus, for whom death involved not only excruciating physical torment, but a spiritual darkness all the blacker for being set against the brightness of unbroken communion with his heavenly Father. It reminds him too of the enormity of the problem from which Christ has released him, relief all too often grossly underrated.

This thought leads to one final point. The underestimate of which we have spoken must surely rank as one of the most crippling factors among those which inhibit Christians from sharing their faith. To read the Book of Job is to catch a glimpse of death as those without Christ must see it. To be alerted to its real horror is to see the horror of living without Christ. Too often, like the writer of Psalm 73, we tend to envy such people as having a surprisingly easy time. Nothing could so quickly alter this illusion as the kind of appreciation that the Book of Job gives that they stand (in spite of things which Job himself uttered) on the most slippery ground, from which they most desperately need to be rescued.

3 Righteousness and self-righteousness

Was Job righteous? This question was fundamental for Job himself. Not only is it also fundamental for the reader seeking to interpret the book, but it leads on to important practical conclusions as the message is applied to the believer's own experience.

That it is a question worth discussing is shown by a recent study of the book by J. H. Kahn, in which he argues that Job's 'perfection' exists only in his own imagination, that it is an obsession which constitutes the real root of his illness, and that the process of cure involves the discovery of his human shortcomings. Kahn's book is full of interest: he relates what he finds in Job to his experience as a practising psychiatrist. And it is significant to notice what may be regarded as a typical response to the Book of Job from an avowedly humanist standpoint.[1]

Yet his analysis goes further than merely translating the ancient account into modern psychological terms. For the basis of the biblical book is not that Job imagined he was righteous, but that he really was. No doubt this assertion needs to be substantiated and clarified, and to this we must now turn. But what is certain is that every major question of interpretation of the Book of Job hangs on what it means to say that Job was righteous, and whether the claim is justified.

1 The meaning of 'righteous'

We might suppose that the question whether or not Job was righteous is answered in the very first verse of the book: 'There lived in the land of Uz a man of blameless and upright life'. But the standard word for 'righteous' (ṣaddîq) is not used here. Nor is it used in verse 8, where God asks Satan whether he has noticed Job; nor at God's second interview with Satan

[1] J. H. Kahn, *Job's Illness: Loss, Grief and Integration*, Pergamon, 1975.

2:3). Is this an accident? The two words which are used have meanings closely similar to that of *ṣaddîq*. The word for 'upright' *(yāšār)* is used to describe terrain as level, not requiring devious paths to traverse. Its exact equivalent in English, likewise used in a moral as well as a physical sense is 'straightforward'. The word for 'blameless' *(tām)*, on the other hand, is used in the Song of Songs (5:2, 6:9) to describe the perfect beauty of the bride; and when this word is transferred to the moral sphere, it refers to a self-consistent, self-authenticating integrity of character.

So perhaps if we could ask the writer why he did not use *ṣaddîq,* he would simply reply, 'I could have done, but is there anything wrong with the words I did use?' Perhaps. But there are reasons for thinking that he deliberately avoided *ṣaddîq* here. Job himself uses the word later (12:4) in a passage which is likely to be intended as a reminiscence of the description of Noah in Genesis 6:9. If, as is probable, the traditional bracketing of the names of Noah and Job as paragons of righteousness was well known to the writer (cf. Ezek. 14:14, 20), it is reasonable to look for an explanation for his constant preference for other words in the Prologue.

The reason is not hard to guess. The whole story of the Book of Job has much in common with a case in a court of law. Job is on trial. And the point about *ṣaddîq* is that the word has very much of a law-court ring about it. If the suspect is cleared in criminal proceedings he is declared *ṣaddîq.* If in what we should call a civil case one party was awarded the verdict, that party would be declared *ṣaddîq*— 'in the right'. So if at the beginning of the Book of Job, the one who was ultimately to emerge as the hero had been declared *ṣaddîq,* the whole logic of the work would have been spoiled. We would know the verdict from the start. It would be as though a judge were to pronounce a prisoner not guilty, and then proceed to hear the case.

But can it be pretended that we do not know the verdict from the start? Surely those adjectives 'blameless' and 'upright' in the mouth of God and in statements of the author himself are enough to settle the matter? It is not so. When God makes

43

his claim about Job to Satan, Satan does not dispute the applicability of these adjectives to Job. What he does is to suggest that a distinction must be made between what Job is like outwardly (outwardly not even Satan can find anything to complain about), and what he is like inwardly. Inwardly, says Satan in effect, we shall be able to tell what he is like if we subject him to certain tests. All that glisters is not gold. Put it in the fire, and the dross will appear. So it will prove in Job's case.

Of course, this is not the only level at which Job is on trial. There is a quarrel at divine cabinet level as to whether Job's outwardly impeccable behaviour is not simply a clever piece of camouflage for extracting favours from God. This is Satan's indictment. But there is also a quarrel at human level between Job and his friends. They take the view that his sufferings prove him beyond doubt to be guilty of grave sins, whereas Job consistently denies that this explanation of his troubles is right.

There is also a third trial in which nobody is involved but Job and God himself. 'Trial' may not be quite the right word for it, because it was more like the small boy's summons to the headmaster's study. But it is important that this third aspect should be clearly distinguished, since otherwise the movement of thought in the book is hard to understand. God has a bone to pick with Job. But it is not the same bone as the friends are picking. Nor is it the same as Satan's. We shall see shortly what that bone was. But before we do so, we must turn to examine the outcome of the other two trials.

2 Satan's indictment

Satan accused Job of being a hypocrite—one who made an outward show of serving God, but whose attitude underneath was impersonal and self-seeking. How did Job fare in the trial on this issue?

It might be thought that if we had only the Prologue and Epilogue it would be plain that Job passed his examination with flying colours, but that the dialogue gives reasons for wondering whether Satan was not proved correct. Some scholars indeed make this the basis for a theory that the two parts of the book are from different hands, and even if there are sound reasons for regarding the present structure of the book as a literary whole, it is undeniable that Job presents us in the work as it stands with a drastic change of mood. 'The Lord gives and the Lord takes away', he has said in an admirable spirit of resignation (1:21, 2:10). But later he inveighs against God in chapter after chapter with a vehemence which, whatever else, cannot possibly be called resigned. So when we find him repenting in dust and ashes at the end of the book, it occurs to us to ask whether we should understand this as a recognition that he had failed the test.

This view cannot be sustained. The end of the book must be interpreted as a vindication of Job—at any rate as far as this fundamental issue, raised by Satan's accusation, is concerned.

This is clear first from what God says about Job in the Epilogue. The friends are rebuked for their wrong attitude in contrast with what God in some respects regards as Job's right attitude (42:7), and, what is more significant, they are invited to seek his help as their intercessor. In the light of such passages as Isaiah 53, effectual intercession is, in Old Testament thought, the hallmark of righteousness.

Secondly, the restoration of Job which then takes place must be seen as evidence of God's vindication of Job. It must not, that is to say, be regarded as evidence that God has *forgiven* Job, as though it were contingent on the repentance of Job recorded in 42:6. If it is contingent on anything, it is the intercession for his friends mentioned above. But this, as we saw, is part and parcel of the overall picture of Job's righteousness, which embraces his life before the drama begins, his behaviour under trial and also this crowning and typical act. It is obvious that God could not have regarded Job as being in the right where the quarrel with his friends was concerned, but in the wrong with regard to the test set up by Satan. We conclude then that Job passed Satan's examination, and that the restoration of his fortunes, with all the round numbers, even rounder than those at the outset, is in the nature of a certificate to this effect.

But it might be felt that this only leaves us with the question *how* Job could be allowed to pass, in view of his performance in the dialogue. There are at least three lines of defence open to an advocate seeking to defend him against the charge that the certificate implied by his restoration was undeserved.

First, Job's undeniable attacks on the justice of God were even at their worst scarcely wholehearted. It is partly that we find them interspersed with assurances that he would at last be vindicated because God is just. Earlier, we saw that his hope of resurrection contained elements of wishful thinking. Here we need to stress the complementary truth that the firm foundation on which that hope arose at all in Job's mind was the ineradicable sense of God's fairness underlying what must be regarded as his more superficial complaints of God's unfairness.

It is partly, on the other hand, that in the same breath as Job complains of God's injustice to him he can let slip out his conviction that God will be just to his friends (13:7–9, 19:29). The guard put up by cynicism drops, and we glimpse the theological undergirding on which his real faith is all the time supported. We can say then that Job's complaints, though not to be excused, were really out of character—false prizes extorted by Satan from his human weakness.

Secondly, Job never envies the wicked. It is a mystery for him, a matter for great grief and misgivings that those who could be credibly regarded as ripe candidates for God's judgement so palpably prospered. But it is vital for an understanding of the thrust of the book to note that Job, when faced in his mind's eye with the choice between righteousness with suffering and ungodliness with prosperity, knows for which he must opt (21:16b).[2]

Thirdly, it is to Job's credit that he is so pertinacious in the discussion. It is true that his pertinacity leads to his making some serious mistakes with his more extreme utterances. For these, as we shall see, God will not excuse him (38:2, 40:2).

---

[2] The NEB follows the Septuagint away from the Hebrew here. But the latter, which reads, 'The counsel of the wicked is far from me' gives clear sense, which is more than can be said, in spite of Dhorme's advocacy, for the alternative.

But it is also the mark of an unrelenting grasp of the truth about God, by which he is sustained throughout his grim ordeal, and for which he duly receives divine praise (42:7). There is no Copernican revolution in Job's stance under pressure. What happens is rather that his fundamental convictions are brought into tension with suggestions and doubts raised by his sufferings. But it cannot possibly be claimed that this tension is resolved by any kind of straightforward abandonment of his faith in God.

3 The friends' indictment

Here we must begin by assessing the attitude of Job's friends at the beginning. Did they believe Job to be a righteous man or not? There is no reason to doubt that they did. After all, they were good at judging the answer to such a question on the basis of the candidate's material prosperity. So since before Job's misfortune began they had no cause to suspect the evidence of God's approval of him, to say the least, we can take it that this must have been their starting-point.

But when did this attitude change? Here the question is less easy, and depends on our interpretation of Eliphaz's first speech. At first sight, it looks as if Eliphaz makes a clear admission of Job's righteousness: 'Is not your fear of God your confidence, and the integrity of your ways your hope?' (4:6 RSV). However, there is a serious difficulty in the way of taking these words at their face value. Eliphaz is going on in verse 17 to declare that no mortal man can be guiltless in God's sight. There is therefore a blatant inconsistency if at one moment Eliphaz tells Job to make his godliness the basis of his sense of security, and at the next he tells him that any such claim is bound to be false!

Of course, the inconsistency could be intentional. One could say that it lays a finger on the basic dilemma of the Pharisee's position, caught as he is between the God he believes in and the necessity, according to his own system, for establishing his own righteousness in God's sight. But it seems better to follow Dhorme's contention that the opening of Eliphaz's speech is ironical.[3] It may seem a drastic expedient thus to have Eliphaz sneering at Job's claim to righteousness, and the friends are painted in more unattractive colours according to such a view. But God makes no qualifications in the rebukes meted out in 42:7. And if Eliphaz is allowed at any point in all seriousness to recognize Job's righteousness before the detailed self-defence in chapter 31, the sharp lines of the drama are blunted. What is more, if irony were foreign to the writer's style, we might hesitate to adopt this solution. But on any reckoning he is very fond of it, and to impute it here seems preferable to the alternative inconsistency.

It follows, if this is a correct analysis, that it was because of what had happened to him that Job's friends regarded him as disqualified in the race for righteousness. No doubt his more colourful outbursts in the course of the discussion served to strengthen their conviction, and fitted in with their assessment that he must have been a hypocrite all along. But it was his sufferings which in their view expressed God's estimate of the man, and thus constituted the primary evidence against him.

They were wrong, of course. That comes across in the book too clearly to need any argument. But a problem arises in the way Job reacts to his friends. Even if he can be acquitted on the kind of charges for which they supposed his sufferings were the punishment, does he not emerge as he answers them with a self-righteousness which counts decisively against him? Particularly if we look at him through New Testament eyes schooled to detect the failings of the Pharisees, it is hard not to sense here a serious drawback for anyone claiming that Job was truly righteous.

Was Job then self-righteous? To say that he had a clear conscience is certainly to put it mildly. The book is well seasoned with his protestations of innocence. These fall into four categories: (i) He complains directly to God:

> Thou knowest that I am guiltless (10:7).

(ii) He complains to his friends of God's injustice;

[3] See p. xxxvi and note to 4:6.

'If he would slay me, I should not hesitate;
I should still argue my cause to his face.
This at least assures my success,
that no godless man may appear before him . . .
Be sure of this: once I have stated my case
I know that I shall be acquitted.

(13:15–18; cf. 16:17 ff., 23:7)

He claims that he is being punished unjustly and that God has denied him justice (19:5–7, 27:1). Finally he makes out a detailed plea in self-defence (31:5 ff.). (iii) He complains of his friends to God:

Thou wilt not let those men triumph,
whose minds thou hast sunk in ignorance;
if such a man denounces his friends to their ruin,
his sons' eyes shall grow dim (17:4–5).

(iv) He complains directly to his friends of their injustice:

I know well what you are thinking
and the arguments you are marshalling against me;
I know you will ask, 'Where is the great man's home now,
what has become of the home of the wicked?' (21:27–8).

The factor which, more than any other, seems to require us to conclude that Job is self-righteous on the strength of this array of evidence is the introduction to Elihu's speeches in 32:1. The New English Bible follows the RSV's interpretation of the Masoretic Text, which reads, 'These three men ceased to answer Job, because he was righteous in his own eyes'. However, there are strong reasons for thinking that the original reading was, 'righteous in their eyes'.[4] But even if the Hebrew

---

[4] These reasons are as follows: (i) This is the reading of Septuagint, Symmachus, Syriac and one Hebrew manuscript, a substantial consensus. (ii) If Job were self-righteous, this would have been an added reason for further contributions from the friends rather than for their silence. Job's claim to have a clear conscience at the outset did not inhibit them. Pope points out (op. cit. p. lxxii, footnote 101) that Job's preparedness to go on oath might have rated in their eyes as tantamount to an acquittal. (iii) This reading would make Elihu's intervention more intelligible (especially

is correct at this point, we need not regard the passage as giving the verdict of the writer. It could perfectly well represent the opinion simply of the friends.

Certainly, Job is rebuked by God. There can be no doubt about that as we read 38:2, 40:2. But what is he rebuked for? We find no indication that the reason is self-righteousness. He has darkened Providence by words devoid of insight. He has been criticizing God. These are things which we shall have to look at in more detail. But even at 40:8, which perhaps comes nearest to a charge of self-righteousness, the stress is on the folly of allowing the condemnation of God to figure in his apologia. God does not accuse Job of falsely claiming to be righteous, and it is very difficult in the face of this to conclude that the writer wished to depict Job as self-righteous.

It may allay some of the misgivings which we feel at this point if we recognize the danger of confusing self-righteousness and self-defence. It is significant that in Job's opening speech in chapter 3, there is no attempt at self-justification. It is only after the innuendos and, in the end, outright accusations that he made his professions of innocence. These do not amount to a claim of sinless perfection. He confesses the sins of his youth (13:26); and it is not that he believes these too trivial to warrant God's notice, but rather, as Davidson says, that he considers them long forgiven. It is reasonable, therefore, to see what Job says as the response of an accused man whose conscience is clear. Both Jesus and Paul provide us with New Testament evidence that it can be on occasion right to speak in one's own defence.

4 God's indictment
However, it is one thing to speak in self-defence to other people, but quite another to do so to God himself. Can we acquit Job at this point? We have seen now that Job was acquitted on two of the counts against him. On the one hand,

if the restoration of 'God' for 'Job' in 32:3 is accepted—see Dhorme's note on the passage). Elihu purports to answer Job's friends as well as Job himself.

Satan's charge was proved to be unfounded: Job's relationship to God went far deeper than the mercenary outlook which his accuser attributed to him. And on the other hand, the friends' conclusion that Job must have been a very wicked man to be suffering so terribly is also shown by the book (and probably admitted by the friends themselves on the strength of Job's oath) to be false. But as we noticed to begin with, God has his own complaint, which is different from the other two issues. Exactly what did it amount to?

It did not concern the question of Job's fundamental relationship with God, which both Satan and the friends impugned. God does not regard Job's claim to righteousness as improper, except for one thing. In the course of his self-defence, Job condemns God. His friends make it clear that they regard his sufferings as penal. Job disagrees with them in the sense that he finds no fault in himself for which they could possibly be regarded as a punishment. But he agrees with the underlying premiss to the extent of saying that since he is not guilty, the sufferings must be a mistake—God's mistake. It is for this that Job is rebuked: not for claiming to be righteous, but for imagining that he had the knowledge necessary for criticizing God's government of the world.

This conclusion is supported by two further considerations. First, the point of the book depends on the knowledge which the reader has, but which is withheld from the protagonists, of what the real reason for Job's sufferings is. All through the dialogue, therefore, there is dramatic irony in the fact that neither Job nor his friends ever come within hailing distance of this ultimate explanation.

Second, the rebuke of God, when it comes, is geared to impress upon Job the limitations not of his righteousness, but his knowledge. A great deal happens, God says, in the world of nature, beyond Job's little ken, which is yet well supervised. Is it not then very unreasonable for Job to criticize? His God, like that which many of us make in our own image, was too small. So when he wakes up to what God is really like—and this is the effect of the theophany in chapters 38–41—Job repents in dust and ashes. His previous knowledge of God seems like a second-hand report; but now, he says, 'I see thee with my own eyes' (42:5).

Yet this is not the day of Job's conversion, except in the sense that every believer needs to be converted again and again in response to ever-expanding views of God's majesty. God restored Job to mark his vindication with outward blessings. But, as we have seen (p. 15), the very roundness of those round numbers emphasizes a crucial point: God had not been mistaken in the first place when he asked Satan, 'Have you considered my servant Job?'

5 Some practical implications

(a) Righteousness involves an inward relationship

Satan was wrong when he suggested that underlying Job's outwardly good behaviour was a heart far from God. But he was not wrong in his perception that if the accusation had been true, God would no longer have been so pleased with Job. Righteousness must certainly fruit in concrete acts of kindness and courage. But its roots are invisible. And what they consist of, if genuine, is a personal regard for God, analogous to a son's love for his father or a bride's for her husband. God is not a source of power to be manipulated impersonally—to think so is precisely what paganism amounts to: he is a person to be relied on and responded to. The reader of *Job* is challenged, therefore, at this point. What would be left of our Christianity if we were to face such a test as Job's? What is the mainspring of the good things which we attempt? Love for God, or love of the earthly pay-off?

(b) Righteousness is impugned and tested

In Job's case the trial was very severe. Christ's was more severe still. But it is not likely that (with this one exception) anyone will ever be able to claim to have been subjected to a more exacting test. Nevertheless, it is made abundantly clear in the Bible that testing comes to those who are righteous. To some Christians the experience comes as a shock, as though it were an inappropriate sequel to their discovery of peace with God. We must look in another chapter at the way in which a Christian should face the problems which this involves. But what the Book of Job teaches us is that not only must one expect testing at two levels, (in the sense that Job's troubles had a spiritual origin in Satan and a range of earthly sources), but also one must not be surprised at being misunderstood and criticized by those, like Job's friends, from whom one might hope to find sympathy and encouragement. The Book of Job is in a sense the map of every Christian's life. From the moment of conversion to our dying day we are on trial.

(c) Righteousness does not imply sinless perfection

To say that righteousness does not imply sinless perfection does not, of course, mean that a believer can look into the future and say, 'I can afford to sin'. But it does mean that he can look into the past with confidence that the falls he has had since becoming a Christian do not destroy his new relationship with God. It is a comfort that the Bible records gross failings of the finest men. Job is no exception. To have established his own innocence at the expense of God's is no minor short-coming. He is rebuked for it in what must rank as the longest sermon in Scripture with God himself as its preacher. But the basic relationship between God and God's servant remains standing, and we may hope that the same will prove true for us when the divine finger is placed critically on the faults that spoil our Christian lives.

(d) Righteousness is vindicated

When Job was sitting on the rubbish dump outside his township scratching his sores, he did not look like anybody that God particularly approved of. Nor did Joseph, stripped and sold to the Ishmaelites; nor David, hounded by King Saul; nor Jesus as he died a criminal's death. And so we could go on, finding many more examples through the length and breadth of the Bible. But a day of reckoning came: a day of earthly restoration, or a day of resurrection. John Wesley lived through an era of abuse and rejection to become in his eighties a figure accorded national respect. Not every Christian who suffers for his faith lives to see such a day on earth. But the Christian looks at Job through New Testament eyes and finds no great difficulty in seeing reflected in Job's ultimate earthly paradise a picture of the investment maturing for all believers in heaven.

4 Depression

Job is an archetype of physical suffering. But the crux of his problem did not lie here. It lay in the question which is posed by his name: 'Where is my father?' Beyond all the bodily anguish with which Job was tormented there was a spiritual problem. 'If only I knew how to find him,' he cried (23:3). The God whom he had known as his friend seemed to have abandoned him: 'Why dost thou hide thy face and treat me as thy enemy?' (13:24).

This means that the Book of Job has a special significance for those who find themselves tortured by precisely this fear. But this does not mean that it is like a bottle of medicine to be kept in the cupboard until one is struck down by the ailment for which it is the specific remedy.

One reason for this is that while spiritual depression is a malady with well-defined characteristics, making the sufferer only too poignantly aware of its presence when it comes to him in its acute form, it is to some extent a constant factor in the day-to-day experience of the believer. For the whole basis of the Christian life lies in the father-son relationship which becomes the believer's privilege through adoption. And while there is on God's side a security about this relationship which nothing can take away, the realization of that security in the believer's experience is another matter. Indeed this is exactly the battleground on which the fight of faith has to be fought. Therefore Job is a handbook not only for the extraordinary battles of the Christian soldier, but for the ordinary ones as well. What is found there depicted as it were in poster colours is reproduced by hourly experience in pastel shades.

But there is another reason why reserving the Book of Job for the moment of crisis is false economy. No doubt it would be misleading to give the impression that one can completely prepare for acute spiritual depression before it arrives. Its unexpected characteristics are partly what make it so agonizing. Nevertheless, anyone who has in a season of clear-shining learned the lessons that the Book of Job has to teach will be much better placed in the struggle to recover faith and assurance when the clouds are dark and menacing than one who has taken it for granted that clear-shining is an ever-present feature of the spiritual climate once one is a Christian. The warfare analogy suggests the obvious point that any manoeuvre of the enemy is less effective if it lacks the element of surprise. But a further reason lies in the fact that spiritual depression often destroys the power of concentration, so that it becomes difficult to read the simplest book or listen attentively to anything that is said.

Jesus himself prepared for his spiritual battle by prayerful meditation on God's word, as is clear from the account of his temptation in the wilderness, and his experience in Gethsemane. It was in the garden there that Jesus won in advance the victory of the cross, no less than Peter and the other disciples lost there the forthcoming battle by sleepy insouciance. And while the kind of trial we are considering here is somewhat different, the need to prepare for it is equally essential.

1 The character of depression
Inability to concentrate takes us into a consideration of some of the features of spiritual depression. This particular characteristic is illustrated clearly enough in the Book of Job. For we find in several of Job's speeches, and more so as the dialogue progresses, that Job is unable to relate to what his friends say to him.

No doubt we must beware of expecting the kind of slick rapport which any modern dramatist would reckon an essential feature of his dialogue, and to some extent the reiteration of his case may be a feature of the ancient Hebrew law-court. Certainly, the Book of Job owes much for its structure and content to the judicial process with which the writer was familiar, whereby both sides went on presenting their own arguments until one was worn down. On the other hand, it is arguable that one of the reasons why the poem is cast in the form of a trial is partly because of the way that the obsessive thoughts of a depressed person fit into precisely this mould, and it is no accident that justification is one of the basic categories in which the Bible presents the salvation of man. At any rate, the plain fact is that Job's replies only turn slowly and obliquely to take account of the points made by his friends.

This must not be regarded as wilful refusal on his part. It is one of the symptoms of this kind of mental illness that the mind becomes dominated by an introverted and recurring train of thought to such an extent that ordinary objective consideration becomes either burdensome or even impossible.

The crucial feature, however, of spiritual depression is the one with which we started: the apparent rupture of one's relationship with God. Amid all Job's problems this was by far the most pressing. He had (from his own point of view) lost God, and this was much more serious than the loss of his material possessions, his relatives or his health. There was a point indeed when all these other things had been taken away but Job had not yet lost his spiritual equilibrium. The time came, however, when God's activity became unintelligible, the sense of communion evaporated, the one who had been his friend now seemed like his enemy, the one to whose presence he had enjoyed a certain access became separated by a yawning gulf. All this is familiar to anyone who has suffered from spiritual depression.

Psychiatrists may find what they view as identical symptoms in both Christians and non-Christians—to them it may seem a matter of small significance that the unbeliever sees, say, money or physical health as the root of his problem, while the believer sees his in terms of the gulf between himself and God. But the particular malady which we are discussing is a distinctively Christian experience. One cannot lose a relationship that has never existed, and it is precisely the fact that there seems to the victim to be a lost relationship which constitutes spiritual depression. This is not to say that something very similar may not accompany the experience which leads up to Christian commitment in the first place. But Job was not 'converted' in this sense in the course of the story. The question of his righteousness is an important and teasing one which we have wrestled with in the previous chapter, but, as we found there, he was at the outset a true believer. While there was much for him to learn from the grim ordeal through which he went, it was not the basic lesson that has to be learned by anyone who makes the step from unbelief to faith. He repented (42:6); but repentance is an essentially ongoing process in the life of a believer, since as a believer one becomes progressively more aware of the problem of sin in all its depth.

It is therefore of the utmost importance to grasp that what Job experienced as a believer may in principle be the experience of any believer. When viewed objectively, therefore, such a trial does not, as some imagine, automatically cast doubt on the genuineness of a person's Christian profession: though, of course, subjectively, it is just this doubt which is the essence of the problem. What is important from a practical point of view is that it is a source of great comfort to anyone in the throes of a depression of this kind to be told: 'This can happen to a true believer'.

Around the central kernel of a God felt to be lost cluster the host of concomitant problems found in the case of Job. The thought of death is never far from the mind of one suffering from spiritual depression. Instead of seeing life in Exodus terms as a purposeful pilgrimage, with God in the lead, from slavery to rest, the depressed man sees himself as one going round and round in meaningless circles in the desert, with neither compass nor friend. And like Elijah, another classic example of a man of outstanding faith who suffered in a similar way, he feels like pleading for his life to be taken away (I Kgs. 19:4).

Yet desire for death can paradoxically go hand in hand with the fear of it. Job remembered the sins of his youth—sins long forgotten because reckoned long forgiven (13:26). For assurance of forgiveness forsakes one who has lost hold of the forgiver, and death resumes its character as punishment, no longer anticipated with the glad confidence of the psalmist as the door to glory (Ps. 73:24 RV).

Guilt, however, is by no means the only reaction. For Job it was not the dominant one. Rather his depression fastened on to the apparently topsy-turvy character of the way in which rewards and punishments are assigned. Again one is reminded of Elijah, depressed not only because he himself was no better than his fathers, but, as the context makes unmistakably clear, because Jezebel was still in the saddle—an outcome of his contest with the priests of Baal which he could not reconcile with his ethical framework. Job too, besides being depressed, was also resentful:

> O that the grounds for my resentment might be weighted,
> and my misfortunes set with them on the scales!
> For they would outweigh the sands of the sea . . . (6 : 2; cf. 23 : 2).

Another common symptom of depression is sleeplessness. Sleep is represented in the Psalms as the gift of God (Ps. 4 : 8; cf. 127 : 2 RV, though NEB regards the text here as corrupt), and even in the most dire trouble, it is possible for believers to sleep calmly (Ps. 3 : 5), as Jesus himself did in the midst of a hair-raising storm (Mk. 4 : 38). Nor is sleeplessness always regarded as having sinister implications, but is several times regarded in the Psalms as an opportunity for profitable meditation (Ps. 63 : 6) or even song (Ps. 77 : 6 RV). Elsewhere, however, the Psalms paint an anguished picture of sleeplessness (Ps. 6 : 6, 77 : 2) and illustrate an aspect of depression which was certainly shared by Job. One passage which expresses his problem in this respect recalls significantly the threats of Deuteronomy (Deut. 28 : 67, Job 7 : 4), and while the sleeplessness Job experienced was no doubt partly due to physical discomfort (30 : 17), it can clearly be counted as a contributory factor in his mental condition.

Finally, there is the sense of humiliation and helplessness which goes with depression. Life itself seems so evanescent, like a mere breath of wind (7 : 7) or dispersing clouds (7 : 9). Job sees himself as lacking strength (6 : 11), with no power to help himself (6 : 13). This is what depression is like. One senses the need to move, to take action, to 'snap out of it'. But it is an integral part of the problem that the power of decision and of purposive action seems to be completely demolished.

2 The cause of depression

Any attempt to analyse the causes of spiritual depression is fraught with a number of difficulties. One is that the condition thrives on a kind of vicious circle, such that various factors which can quite properly be regarded as symptoms soon find a place in any list of causes. Sleeplessness is a good example. On the one hand, it is not until one becomes a prey to the kind of anxious thoughts that go with depression that one begins seriously to lose sleep; on the other, failure to have proper rest may often be a highly significant reason why spiritual depression progresses to an acute stage.

A further problem is that there are various levels of causation. One can analyse any particular case of depression from a spiritual point of view, or what we may call a historical point of view, or even a biochemical point of view. And the kind of factors which will count as causes under these headings are not necessarily in conflict with one another: indeed, one ought to think rather of a hierarchy of causes operating at different levels.

In an earlier chapter we dealt at some length with the part played by Satan in the Book of Job, and gave reasons for taking seriously the attribution of such evils to him. But Satan's part in creating suffering can perhaps be likened to the power that an author has in moulding the events and characters in a novel. Or if this seems too much like putting him in the place of God himself, perhaps we should see him rather as a kind of wicked sub-editor. The point is that he is to be seen as operating at a different level of causation from any of the other factors which have to be noticed; as is perfectly clear from the Prologue, where we find that Satan appears 'in person' at the divine cabinet level, while his objectives are carried out in earthly terms in a way which is susceptible of *historical* analysis.

The weapons which Satan uses are seen first of all in the kinds of external troubles which beset Job: the loss of his possessions, bereavement and physical disease. These are typical examples of a large range of factors capable of triggering off depression. But in fact Satan was robbed of his expected success as a result of this kind of frontal assault, and it was only through Job's friends that he achieved a measure of success. This is not spelt out in the book, but there is a startling contrast between the resignation of Job before the arrival of his friends and his breakdown after it—a contrast which constitutes an important feature of the plot as the book stands. And for the possibility of Satan's using a man's friends to war against him, we need look no further for biblical example than to Jesus's rebuke of Peter, 'Get thee behind me, Satan' (Mk. 8:33).

However this may be, Job's disappointment in his friends represents a common and potent cause of depression: when those whom we trust most let us down worst—particularly if the disappointment comes, as it did in Job's case, not so much in anything done or said against us as in a fundamental misjudgement of our character. To be slandered by our enemies is predictable and to that extent can be tolerated. But to be misunderstood by our friends, not in any trivial matter, but one which goes to the roots of what we are, can be a heart-breaking shock. Nothing expresses this more vividly than Job's comparison of himself to a desert traveller, who sees what looks in the distance like a mountain stream; he leaves his track in the hope of water; he winds his way through the wilderness to find it; but when he arrives the torrent has gone dry; it was his last chance of survival; no other oasis is within range to save him (6:14-20).

Finally, there was himself. Modern psychiatry draws a distinction between what it calls endogenous and exogenous depressions. An endogenous depression is one which cannot be accounted for by factors outside of the patient himself, while an exogenous one can. Job would be a classic example of the latter kind, since one can easily discover in his case just the sort of disasters which are often responsible for bringing on depression. But the distinction is not clear-cut. On the one hand, a man suffering from what a psychiatrist would regard as an endogenous depression may well attribute his problems to something quite definite. He may for instance feel that the root of his trouble is guilt for some past sin. Anyone else, hearing about it, may feel that the matter concerned is so trivial or so far buried in the past that it must be a rationalization. But such an analysis is singularly unhelpful to the victim, for to him the anguish of guilt is as much the underlying cause of his depression as the financial disaster that brings similar symptoms to somebody else. The truth is that every depression has both exogenous and endogenous aspects, so that while the balance between the two may vary from one case to another, the distinction is never an absolute one.

Thus Job's depression may have been mainly due to external factors. But it would be a mistake to pay no attention to what we may call his own contribution. The fear of death, the sense of bewilderment, of injustice, or of God's abandonment come unsolicited. But whenever such feelings arise in our minds, the will becomes involved. And it is here that the Book of Job serves as an accurate mirror in which to examine ourselves. For while we cannot avoid feelings, we are responsible for settled attitudes. Feelings come uninvited, but depend for survival on our entertaining them. So with Job. The sense that God had abandoned him was an unavoidable element in his trouble. But for that feeling to become a ruling factor in what he did and said needed the permission of his will. This may sound all too much like adopting the position of the arm-chair critic. However, it is one of the major themes of the Book of Job to show how he concluded too soon that God had abandoned him. His mistake is therefore a powerful beacon for us, who mostly come to the same conclusion much sooner and on much slenderer evidence.

Of course, it is cold comfort to say to someone who is depressed that his depression could have been avoided. It may indeed be false as well as cruel. But there is a practical lesson to draw at this point: the best place to check the enemy is at the gate; once he has obtained access to the city, the battle becomes much more complex. A believer may certainly find himself involved in the second kind of warfare, as many of the

Psalms bear witness, but the Christian soldier has so to learn to use the shield of faith that the fiery arrows of doubt can be quenched before they can do serious damage.

3 The remedy for depression
There are various ways in which the Book of Job affords help in coping with depression. Firstly, there are negative lessons to be learned from Job's mistakes, which, either implicitly or explicitly, the book corrects. Then there are positive lessons to be learned from Job's victorious emergence from his trial. Thirdly, there are lessons which are independent of Job's good or bad example, but which are taught by the outcome of the book as a whole. And, finally, there are lessons to be drawn from the consideration of the privileged position of a Christian in contrast with the limitations of Job's theological horizon.

(a) Lessons from Job's mistakes
It might seem rather unfair to start here with the charge that Job made mistakes in the way he reacted to his friends. Did they not ask for it? Of course, the balance of blame here leans heavily in their direction. On the other hand, one cannot altogether dissociate Job's querulous attitude to God from his querulous attitude to his friends. They were, after all, in spite of all their shortcomings, seeking to help him. They were, unlike Job's other acquaintances, at least there when his day of trouble came. And one only needs to consider the way in which Jesus or Stephen behaved towards those who made no pretence to be friends to see the high standards which grace sets for the behaviour of believers under pressure. Unfortunately, however, when one reflects how easily mere trifles make us lose our cool with others, our glasshouses are too fragile for us to start throwing stones at Job.

Yet two facts remain. One is that if we are less than gracious to those who seek to help us, we set limits on the help they can give us. Job found the silence of his friends trying and their opening speeches more trying; but it was partly his own provocative responses which rendered their ultimate utterances quite unbearable. The actual experience of depression makes this advice far from easy to follow when the moment comes, but it is very important nevertheless to remember that the friendship of others is the most potent medicine for depression, and all the stronger when the patient recognizes the fact and does his best to be receptive to what his friends have to offer.

The other fact is an aid to that. It is only realistic to expect that some of the friends of a depressed man will suggest repentance as their solution for his problems. There is no excuse for this when the Book of Job stands as a biblical embargo on offering this solution when the only evidence for sin in the victim's life is the symptoms of depression. But it is better to be warned: it is likely to happen. For Job it was a shock when he found his friends imputing his troubles to his failings. But if it comes as no surprise, the pain which it causes is at any rate easier to cope with.

The second negative lesson is that Job's protestations of innocence were unproductive. To establish the fact that they were unproductive is part of the dramatic purpose of Elihu's speeches. Their presence and length make the point that Job was not vindicated the moment he had taken an oath to repudiate his friends' charges. He was vindicated in God's good time. There was a sense in which Job's protestations of innocence had to be unproductive; otherwise the terms of the test which Satan insisted on would have been unfulfilled. But the real point is that they were in fact *irrelevant*. If Job were being punished, his innocence would have been important. Since, however, his sufferings were neither retributive nor corrective, his innocence was not in question. This has important implications for the Christian. For the Christian's sufferings also are not necessarily retributive or corrective in character. Like Job's, they serve a purpose which God does not wholly disclose. The particular point at which mystery persists is why one Christian is called on to suffer so much more grievously than another. But the Book of Job shows that, whatever the answer to this mystery turns out to be, it is not because one Christian deserves to suffer more than another. Therefore, when crisis comes, it discourages (provided there is no *reason* to believe that we have brought trouble upon ourselves) the natural reaction, 'What have I done to deserve this?'

Thirdly, we come to the mistake which is specifically corrected in the book by the rebuke which God administers. We must grapple with this in more detail at a later stage. Here it must suffice to point out that God's sermon had one main point: to make clear to Job that his fundamental error was the assumption that he could see the whole picture. Based on this assumption was his criticism that God's government of the world was sadly inadequate—with upright men consigned, as he was, to the rubbish dump, while those who snapped their fingers at God rose to the heights of prosperity. God did not, by way of answer to this, tell Job the whole story as it is revealed to the reader at the outset. Rather he made Job recognize from the limitations of his own experience even in the natural world with which he was familiar that there was overwhelming evidence of God's control.

(b) Lessons from Job's triumph

Job is proverbial, of course, for his patience. And like many English proverbs, the 'patience of Job' derives from the Authorized Version. But one needs to probe further. Job was already proverbial for something by the time James wrote his epistle (Jas. 5:11). The question is whether 'patience' is the right word. The Greek word in that passage is *hupomonē*, and its meaning is defined in the context by the quotation from Dan. 12:12, which James has just cited: 'We count those happy who stood firm (*tous hupomeinantas*)'. The word *hupomonē* is often used in the New Testament, notably in Rom. 2:7, 5:3–4. No English word quite reproduces its flavour. 'Patience' is too passive. 'Endurance' is better (RV mg). But both words are too psychological; as though what was being described were the traditional English virtue of the stiff upper lip! The Emperor Nero once made an unsuccessful attempt on his mother's life, by sending her to sea in a ship with holes in the bottom. Robinson's classic description of her escape— 'Somehow the indomitable lady managed to keep afloat!'—

suggests the idea that was in James' mind: 'unsinkability' would have the right logic if such a word existed.

We conclude then that although Job is proverbial for his patience, the proverb originated from a misunderstanding. This is a considerable relief to the expositor. For while Job's resigned spirit in the Prologue makes it easy to sustain a claim that he was patient up to the end of chapter 2, the dialogue presents us with the picture of a man who was patient neither with God nor with his friends. But he was unsinkable. When James' accolade is properly understood, it is one which is based on a fair summary of the Book of Job as a whole.

This does not mean that Job can be cheaply excused for the way in which he behaved, or that a Christian does not have (as we noticed above) a more exacting model even than him when it comes to facing grievous suffering. But it has something to say to us when we find ourselves to a greater or lesser degree standing in Job's shoes. The important thing to notice is that all was not lost when Job thought it was lost. Not only did he escape from sufferings when he expected them to issue swiftly in death itself. The point here is rather that God restored Job after he had capped his sense of God's abandonment by saying things calculated to finalize the breach in the relationship. It is possible for us to say things which in our own view mark the death of faith, but which God is not blinded by, since he knows that living roots of true belief lie grounded in the heart so deep that we ourselves cannot apprehend them.

We should take comfort from Job's survival. For it may be that when we match the extent of our rebellion with his we find less reason for despairing than he had. Certainly the saints must persevere. But there is a danger for some of imagining that perseverance means riding to heaven on the crest of a spiritual wave, and being disappointed when their Christian experience does not follow this pattern. Paul and Barnabas knew better. They warned their converts that to enter the kingdom of God we must pass through many hardships (Acts 14:22). And these hardships are not only external problems such as rabid persecution. The warning equally embraces such mundane things as failure in the important examination, difficulties in courtship (even with the right person), parental opposition, financial hardship—all those things which we might lightly think that as Christians we have a right to be spared, not the least of which is the struggle faith undergoes to remain buoyant when God seems far away.

(c) Lessons from the outcome of the book as a whole

Up to now we have been concerned with unsinkability as a description of Job's own attitude. In spite of all the trials which he had to endure, there were crucial points at which he did not give in. He made great mistakes; but when it came to the kind of evidence which Satan wanted to prove his thesis that Job's love for God was ultimately a matter of self-interest, he stopped short. He stopped short although the end was not in sight, although vindication was not a matter of present experience but the substance of future hope—and pretty wistful hope at that.

But the reader can understand Job's unsinkability not so much as a description of his attitude as a statement of fact: Job was not sunk. This goes beyond Job's vices and virtues to make what is perhaps the most important point of all. There is an end to the dark tunnel. There is an end to it, not because of anything that the believer can do; by himself he can do nothing. There is an end to the tunnel because Satan's power of temptation is restricted to what the believer can bear; because the believer is in God's hand and nothing can take him out of it. The pages of the Bible are well-stocked with examples of believers who had to go through dark tunnels. But every one had its end. And the end of so many dark tunnels described in Scripture is the guarantee that there will be an end to this one, or to the next one that has yet to be endured.

(d) Lessons from a Christian perspective

The Christian is not meant to read the Book of Job in a vacuum, but rather to see it in its context not only in the Old Testament, but in the Bible as a whole. There are points at which Jesus provides an answer to the cries of Job, and we close this chapter by examining two examples of this.

One of Job's forlorn hopes is for a mediator or umpire; someone who could stand between himself and God and deal with both on equal terms (9 : 33). For a Christian this need is answered. He has in Christ a high priest able to sympathize with his weaknessess, and in the Holy Spirit one who can interpret his prayers in the presence of God.

Another desperate demand which Job makes is for vindication: it is something which would compensate for the loss of all else. But for a Christian, vindication (or justification) can in one sense be a present experience. The message which Job wanted to see engraved in rock so that it could never be erased or forgotten the Christian sees engraved on the wounded hands of Christ, held out to him as the token of God's acquittal.

Of course, the existence of Christian answers is not a complete panacea for the depressed man. He may have a thorough head-knowledge of them all, and yet feel that they apply to everybody except himself. This is a classic symptom of spiritual depression. But it is a great mistake to think that it renders valueless the application of sound Christian teaching. The counsellor who uses such teaching wisely can accomplish two things.

In the first place he can counter the wild assertions of the one whom he is seeking to help, and even in his moments of deepest depression check their sometimes suicidal tendencies; as though Christian doctrine were like the walls of a padded cell from which the patient recoils without doing himself any harm.

In the second place, the counsellor can see himself as building a house for the patient to live in. The trouble to begin with is that he has no key to let himself in. But there is always the hope that sometime he will find it; then suddenly that house which seemed only to exist in wonderland will become real and accessible. What is the key? The best place to look for it is in the promise of Jesus that ultimately the Holy Spirit is never withheld from those who seek from God this, the most precious of all his gifts (Lk. 11 : 9–13). He alone can make the truths of Scripture live, and he will do it.

5 The intellectual problem

The mere experience of physical pain or spiritual desolation presents the believer with a problem. But this is greatly increased when it is complicated by the question, 'Why is this happening to me?' This question is of central interest in the Book of Job, and Job's friends are there to highlight it. For in their mouths are two attempts at an answer. These, we can be sure, enjoyed a wide measure of acceptance in the community to which the Book of Job was addressed, and the writer himself saw they contained a considerable element of truth. Nevertheless, one of his objectives is to expose them as inadequate.

It is sometimes said that the Book of Job is one of the world's finest descriptions of the human predicament, but ends without offering any solution to the intellectual problem of suffering. This conclusion may appeal to the resigned mood of some contemporary philosophy but it does not do justice to the writer of Job. For it is our aim to show that he presents not one answer, but a range of answers to the problem with which he grapples.

However, it is the writer's method to advocate these answers against the backcloth of those proposed by Job's friends, and to let the most distinctive aspect of his solution emerge phoenix-like from the dying embers of Job's dialogue with them. Here too we shall follow the same pattern, looking first at the inadequate answers, and then moving on to a statement of the book's positive contribution.

1 Retribution

Let us begin by disposing of an over-simplified version of the friends' position. Suppose their argument were of the form:

> (a) The tradition promises misfortune to those who maltreat widows, orphans, etc.

(*b*) Job is suffering such misfortune.
Therefore
(*c*) Job is guilty of maltreating widows, orphans etc.

If this were the case, any primary school child, armed as nowadays with a Venn diagram, could expose the logical fallacy. For it would be exactly the same kind of error as the following:

(*a*) All cats scratch.
(*b*) This animal scratches.
Therefore
(*c*) this animal is a cat.

But the matter is not as simple as this. Take first the term 'the tradition'. The friends, particularly Bildad (8:8–10), claim to be speaking for age-long wisdom—a tradition now revealed by archaeological research to have had an immensely long history in the Near-Eastern milieu in which the Old Testament arose. This tradition has left its mark on Scripture, obviously enough in Proverbs (one part of which is virtually identical with its parallel in the Egyptian wisdom book of Amenemope[1]), less obviously in Deuteronomy and the Prophets. But the controversial question how far the element of borrowing extends is one which we can by-pass here, since the writer of the Book of Job takes it for granted, himself one of the latest contributors to the Old Testament (most scholars believe), that there is no practical distinction between the teaching of tradition, to which the friends of Job refer, and the message of Old Testament wisdom embodied in Scripture. The scene may be set hundreds of years before there was any such thing as Scripture, but this does not alter the fact that the writer is using this dramatic form to debate matters of biblical interpretation.

Look then at Deuteronomy. It provides a very clear statement of the theological principles upon which the friends' outlook was based, and its contents were certainly influential in the whole conception and structuring of Job. But it does not

[1] Prov. 22:17–23:11. Compare G. von Rad, 'Wisdom in Israel' (ET J. D. Martin, SCM 1972), p. 9 and works cited in note 5.

simply promise misfortune for disobedience to God. It promises also blessings for obedience.

This rules out the possibility of faulting the friends on a matter of elementary logic, and the question resolves itself into how the sufferings of Job can be consistent with the reliability of biblical teaching.

The friends have their cut and dried answer. According to them there is no inconsistency. Deuteronomy is an accurate spiritual thermometer. Job is suffering greatly. Indeed his sufferings fit with uncanny exactitude the terms of punishment which that book threatens. Measured by Deuteronomy, therefore, Job must be a great sinner.

Now if this answer were satisfactory, there would be no intellectual problem to resolve. But clearly the Book of Job, whether or not this is where its main thrust lies, is a counterblast against this point of view. G. von Rad warns his readers that the modern mind finds it difficult to feel the sense of sympathy which the original readers of Job would have had with the friends' outlook, and suggests that the balance in favour of Job would to them have looked less clear.[2] While there is a measure of truth in this, two things must be said. First there can be no doubt that the writer, though prepared to give the friends' theology the kind of hearing that it may not so easily receive today, has the criticism of that theology as one of his aims. Second, the idea that the friends' point of view is a relic of the past can be greatly exaggerated in deference to Western university circles. In the experience of the present writer, the theology of Job's friends is very much alive, not only in Yorubaland, but in Yorkshire—just as it was in Palestine in Jesus' day, when he was asked, 'Who sinned, this man or his parents, that he was born blind?' (Jn. 9:2 RSV).

One alternative is that the writer is debunking the biblical tradition, and presenting a theology to supersede Deuteronomy. However, this explanation involves either severe surgery for the text of Job, or the theory that the book as it stands is a composite document without any theological consistency. Both

[2] Op. cit., p. 217.

beginning and end unquestionably give the writer's endorsement to what we may call the deuteronomic standpoint: Job's
initial prosperity reflected the righteousness with which he was
credited in the first verse, and his ultimate prosperity reflects
his vindication by God at the end.

Is there then a third possibility, which neither falls into the
error of Job's friends, nor requires the rejection of Deuteronomy? It is our thesis that this is precisely how the intellectual problem was formulated by the writer of Job, and that his
book was intended to answer it.

At the outset, one must give full weight to the biblical support that Job's friends could muster. If Eliphaz were challenged, he could reply (if we overlook the anachronism) that the
line he was taking was not very different from that of Ezekiel's
sermon to his people:

> As I live, says the Lord God, I have no desire for the death of
> the wicked. I would rather that a wicked man should mend his
> ways and live. Give up your evil ways, give them up; O Israelites,
> why should you die? (Ezek. 33:11).

Or he might go to the Book of Proverbs and say that his
message to Job is only the kind of thing that he could read
there:

> To do right is the protection of an honest man,
> but wickedness brings sinners to grief (Prov. 13:6).

Or he could say that he and his friends have been strictly
faithful to the message of Deuteronomy in everything they
have said to Job.

The writer does not answer these hypothetical objections
directly. But his own position depends on the possibility of
answering them, and consideration of the problem in this way
may be expected to show us where to look for his own solution.

Let us then take these three biblical defences one by one,
in order to see why they are not adequate to justify the friends'
approach to Job.

Why was it legitimate for Ezekiel to put before his congregation the hope of restoration which might be expected to result from repentance, but wrong for Job's friends to do the same? The answer must be that in Ezekiel's case there was no doubt about the people's guilt of those sins for which the Babylonian exile was the grievous punishment. He was not making the mistake of inferring from the mere fact of the people's sufferings the charge that they had sinned. There was other clear and undeniable evidence of their guilt. But this kind of evidence was what Job's friends lacked. To have pursued their case for the prosecution without it was itself an offence against Deuteronomy and this alone should have given them pause.

Suppose then they were to argue that their basic model was the approach of the Book of Proverbs. Here was a book clearly addressed to the individual believer. Why should it not be in order to apply its teaching to someone in Job's position? Here a very important principle of interpreting Scripture comes into play. It is not enough to be guided by the actual words of the text: attention also needs to be given to their life-situation. The Book of Proverbs is a work of foundation ethics. It is not, as is the case with Ezekiel's sermon, addressed to people in a particular position. To illustrate the point, take the English proverb, 'Too many cooks spoil the broth'. If this is uttered in anticipation of any soup-making, it offers *advice*. But if it is uttered when the soup is already ruined, then it pronounces *condemnation*. Now this second type of application may not be always out of place. But in order to be apposite, it needs to be supported by evidence. But evidence of the right kind is exactly what Job's friends did not have, as we saw when we were examining their first possible line of defence. The approach of Proverbs, therefore, does not provide them with an adequate model for addressing Job as they did. For we can accuse them either of illegitimately transferring this kind of message into a context in which it is not appropriate, or of lacking the kind of evidence necessary for making it appropriate.

But it may be felt that this still fails to reach the heart of the problem. And if Job's friends could answer us back at this point, they would say, 'None of these subtleties alters the plain facts of the case. Deuteronomy promises blessings to the righteous, misery to the disobedient. Job is suffering in precisely the way Deuteronomy threatens. It follows that either Job is sinful, or (*per impossibile*) Deuteronomy is unreliable.' This then is the case to be answered. We can call it the retributive theory of suffering.

2 Correction

Before we go on to see what answer the Book of Job gives to this position, it will be as well to examine at this stage a rather different line of argument which Job's friends also put forward.

Its main exponent is Elihu. He is the younger man who has waited throughout the dialogue until at length his seniors fall silent. Some think that his speeches are later additions to the book. Others (for instance M. H. Pope[3]) think that Elihu is the mouthpiece for the main thrust of the writer's message. Here we have the most finely chiselled couplets; here, we are told, all the writer's rhetorical skill is displayed, as though the heaviest artillery had been saved up for this crucial campaign. But while there is no doubt a danger of bringing from modern Western taste wrong criteria to bear on matters of style, it does seem difficult to avoid the impression that the writer is mocking Elihu. The young man is self-confessedly angry:

> For I am bursting with words,
> a bellyful of wind gripes me.
> My stomach is distended as if with wine,
> bulging like a blacksmith's bellows (32:18f.).

He is unbelievably pompous and patronizing:

> 'Come now, Job, listen to my words' (33:1).

> 'Listen, Job, and attend to me' (33:31).

[3] Op. cit., p. 213.

74

'Was there ever a man like Job
with his thirst for irreverent talk' (34: 7).

'Now, Job, if you have the wit, consider this' (34:16).

This is not how young men were expected to address their
elders in patriarchal times! Nor were they supposed to speak
at such immoderate length. It is part of the writer's joke that
Elihu makes not one speech but four, with scarcely a token
pause for his hearers' reaction. These points would be by themselves sufficient to make it clear that he is not intended to be
the writer's vehicle for the right answer. But there is a further
thing. Elihu's main contention is that the purpose of suffering
is disciplinary:

To turn a man from reckless conduct,
to check the pride of mortal man,
at the edge of the pit he holds him back alive
and stops him from crossing the river of death.
Or again, man learns his lesson on a bed of pain,
tormented by a ceaseless ague in his bones . . .
All these things God may do to a man,
again and yet again,
bringing him back from the pit
to enjoy the full light of life (33 : 17ff.).

From Elihu's manner, one would gather that this solution is a
fresh idea, not mentioned previously in the dialogue at all.
But this is not the case. At the outset, Eliphaz has clearly
enunciated the disciplinary theory of suffering:

Happy the man whom God rebukes!
therefore do not reject the discipline of the Almighty (5:17).

How then are we to interpret Elihu's contribution? It does
not seem to carry the writer's endorsement; nor is he saying, in
spite of his pretensions, anything new. These facts certainly
present difficulties for the view that Elihu's speeches are a
later addition. But they leave to be explained their inordinate

length and their undeniable polish. The answer which raises fewest difficulties is that, far from being the writer's mouthpiece, Elihu is the one whose position he particularly wanted to demolish. It may be that the disciplinary theory had become fashionable as a sophisticated alternative to the retributive. If so, the writer is making the point that not only is it anything but new, but it is also no more satisfactory. In this way, the writer brings to a climax the case for his opponents, using Elihu to summarize what he regarded as an unsatisfactory solution, but doing so in the most forceful and impressive way. For Elihu is far from being altogether a cartoon figure regarded by the writer as talking wholly nonsense. There is a large measure of truth in, and scriptural support for, the case which Elihu marshals. But while it purports to be an all-embracing philosophy of suffering that he offers, Job is the rock on which Elihu's ship, like those of Job's other friends, must founder.

3 The writer's solution

If our quest is for the book's distinctive thrust, the most obvious place to look is the discourse in the mouth of God himself. True, there is at least one scholar who thinks that the only possible way of interpreting God's speeches is as a parody![4] But while irony is a weapon which the writer knew well how to use, it seems simply too clever to suppose that he might carry it to these lengths, especially when no really satisfying or self-consistent exegesis of the book emerges from this kind of interpretation.

Let us assume then that God's words in the book are to be taken seriously. What is their message? The first thing to notice is that God's words are addressed to Job. That is, they are spoken to the spiritual need of the sufferer, and only secondarily to the intellectual need of the reader. We shall be looking more thoroughly at God's speeches in a later chapter, but since they play an unquestionable part in the writer's overall answer to the problem of suffering, the matter must be treated briefly here.

[4] George Bernard Shaw similarly interprets them as a sneer in *The Black Girl in Search of God*, Penguin, p. 19.

It is because the divine speeches do not concern themselves with any philosophical solution to the intellectual problem that some have supposed that the Book of Job as a whole offers no answer of this kind. This is a mistake. The sufferer's fundamental need is for the maintenance or recovery of his communion with God. This is threatened by the sense of desolation caused by the thought that God must have lost control to allow such things to happen to his faithful servants. The message of God's sermon to Job, therefore, is that one needs only to lift one's eyes away from the storm-tossed scene of one's own life to the panorama of the created universe to see that there is overwhelming evidence that God is still on the throne. The sermon is thus an appeal for continued trust. There is no answer to the question, 'Why is this happening to Job?' except in so far as Job is rebuked for concluding that it is because either God's power or wisdom has failed.

This in itself is an important qualification and has to be entered in the ledger as a contribution to solving the intellectual problem. But this is by no means all that is offered. Part of the answer comes not at the end, but at the beginning. For the Prologue does provide, what God's sermon does not, a reason for Job's devastating experience. What is made clear there is that Job's sufferings are not in any sense either retributive or corrective. Their purpose is to vindicate. But whom do they vindicate? It is not only Job: for God's honour too is involved. Satan's slanderous suggestion implies a slur on both partners in the relationship which he criticizes. If he had turned out to be right, Job would have been proved a hypocrite. But God would have been proved a fool. The characters of both were at stake.

Yet is this all the writer says? If it were, we should certainly have to admit that he does not fully answer the intellectual problem in the form in which he poses it. For as soon as one takes the dialogue into account, as well as the prose framework of the book, the way in which the question insists on phrasing itself is, 'What about Deuteronomy?' How can the sufferings of Job be consistent with biblical ethics?

One approach which is worth exploring, although it will

prove to be a *cul de sac* is this. It might be argued that Deuteronomy is the charter for a nation, rather than an address to the individual. A number of modern philosophers have objected to the way in which Christians, when faced with evidence that right-living individuals suffer rather than prosper, seek to escape by saying that while *outwardly* such people seem to be in trouble, they are *in reality* all right.[5] Similarly, anyone unsympathetic to the view that the ethical sanctions of Deuteronomy can be taken seriously today may argue that it is not fair to spiritualize its message by claiming that the believer can never be robbed of a certain 'inner prosperity'. The New Testament will not permit any surrender to such strictures, for its writers constantly resort to the consolation that suffering Christians are better off than appearances suggest (Rom. 8:35–39, Mt. 5:3, Jn. 16:33), and this does in a sense amount to spiritualizing Deuteronomy's message. Now an attempt could be made to explain this by restricting the sense in which Deuteronomy's material promises are to be understood to *national* prosperity.

It is true, as the history of Israel reminds us, that for Deuteronomy to fit even the facts of national life, one needs to allow for a time-lag before God's word is fulfilled. His mill, as the proverb has it, grinds slowly. But the burden of the Old Testament narrative is that Israel, first the Northern Kingdom and then Judah in the south, proved by bitter experience the relevance and truth of Deuteronomy's teaching. What had happened to the Canaanites happened to them too. For they ignored the warnings not to do what the Canaanites did. And every nation is subject to God's law. There is a correlation between the rise and fall of civilizations and the extent to which they reflect its elementary principles of morality: so that to one who sees the flagrant idolatry, the preoccupation with the occult, and the sexual deviance of present-day society, Deuteronomy gives reason for trembling.

In this way it might be argued that Deuteronomy is strictly applicable to nations, but that it is a mistake to expect its

[5] See, e.g. A. G. N. Flew, *New Essays in Philosophical Theology*, SCM, 1955, pp. 275 ff.

pattern of blessings and curses to work itself out in the life of the individual.

But while there certainly are important distinctions to be made in the application of Scripture to nations and individuals, this line of argument is not satisfactory. Other books, particularly Proverbs and Psalms, apply Deuteronomic teaching to the individual. And what are we to say of such a case as Job's? That there must be exceptions to prove the rule? That God's promises have only a statistical reliability comparable with cholera vaccine? It has to be admitted that the Book of Job does not encourage any such solution; any more than there is the slightest suggestion in it that the writer sees the key in the fact that Job is an individual and not a nation.

There is only one alternative. What the book depicts is not the abandonment or rejection of Deuteronomic principles of reward and punishment, but their *suspension*. The beginning and the end emphasize the ordinary outworking of these principles, in such a way that there can be no question of interpreting the book, as some wish to do, as a radical criticism of Deuteronomy itself. What is criticized is the friends' use of Deuteronomy, and in particular their failure to make allowances for the possibility of the kind of suspension that the situation of Job is intended to illustrate.

But how are we to understand this suspension? Let us look first at an analogy from purely human behaviour. When Herod was asked for the head of John the Baptist, the right thing would have been to refuse. If he had done so, he would not have abandoned the rule that one ought to keep one's promises: he would have exemplified the principle that there are situations in which a higher law takes precedence. Jesus makes exactly this point when dealing with those who evaded their responsibility to parents on pretence of loyalty to promises (Mk. 7:9-13). In Job the higher law is clear enough to see: it is more important to vindicate the reality, the depth, the indissoluble spirituality of the relationship between God and the believer than its material profitability.

A complementary approach takes its starting point from an interesting definition of grace quoted by G. Bornkamm:

As was well said by G. Radbruch, 'Grace is most closely related to miracle. As miracle breaks the laws of nature, grace breaks the laws of law . . .'

And Bornkamm comments: 'Grace does not jeopardize the order imposed by law, nor does it cancel out the distinction between good and evil and lead to anarchy. It establishes a new order, the new covenant.'[6]

But the preparedness of the believer to suffer rather than turn his back on God is the reflection of grace. It too is a miracle in the realm of moral law comparable with any suspension of natural law. It is in this light that one can understand the New Testament's conviction that suffering is even to be considered a privilege (Rom. 5:3, Jas. 1:2) since it exhibits the character of Christian faith as nothing else can do.

Of course, not all Job stories have the happy ending that we find in the biblical book. But this could scarcely have escaped the writer; nor can we easily believe that he had no message for situations which ended without any earthly restoration. What the message is we are hardly left to guess. Job won through to the faith that he would be vindicated sooner or later: if not here, then somehow hereafter. For Job it turned out to be sooner. But for similarly placed readers for whom it turns out not to be sooner, the Book of Job preaches the hope that at least it will be later. For those who can see their suffering as a suspension of God's benefits but not of his concern are those who 'through faith' possess 'the assurance of things hoped for' (Heb. 11:1 RSV). The message which the early Christians saw shining in full-orbed glory in the risen Christ had a glimmering dawn in the latter days of Job. For Jesus, like Job, was restored on earth in order to give assurance to others of restoration in a greater light and upon another shore.

We cannot agree therefore with those who accuse the writer of leaving the intellectual problem of suffering unanswered. His book must indeed be read as a critique of two attempts at an answer which he rejects. But he is not guilty of failure to erect a replacement for the buildings he demolishes. There

6 *Paul* (ET D. M. G. Stalker), Hodder 1971, p. 141.

is no denial that some suffering is retributive, or that some is corrective. But it is insisted that these explanations are not exhaustive, and that there is a third factor which operates— what we here call the principle of suspension.

On the other hand, such suspension of the normal outworking of godliness in prosperity is not due to divine fickleness or inefficiency; it is due rather to the believer's participation in a battle which is being fought out at a supernatural level, the details of which can only be hinted at, or described in picturesque terms, so that in the nature of the case the sufferer can never have concrete evidence of it.

In their understanding both of the sufferings of Christ and of Christians the New Testament writers effectively endorse what the Book of Job teaches. No doubt the resurrection allows them to ink in the framework which is barely sketched by the Book of Job with mere earthly shadows. But for those who complain that the New Testament has little to say on the intellectual problem of suffering, the answer may well be that there was nothing to add to its definitive treatment here in the Old.

6 The failure of human sympathy

A careful reading of the gospel narrative shows us that one of the most poignant ordeals undergone by Jesus was the failure of his friends to stand by him. What Satan was unable to achieve in the frontal assault of the wilderness temptations he sought to accomplish in the guise of those closest to him. Not only are we told that Satan entered into Judas Iscariot at the moment of betrayal (Jn. 13:27), but even Peter, for attempting to deflect Jesus from his mission, draws upon himself the rebuke, 'Away with you, Satan' (Mk. 8:33). But this was not a game at which Satan was playing for the first time, but rather an art in which he was highly skilled. Jeremiah experienced it (Jer. 20:10); and so did the Psalmist, who gives classic expression to his disappointment in the words:

> Even the friend whom I trusted, who ate at my table,
> exults over my misfortune (Ps. 41:9).

The failure of friendship is an aspect of suffering no less important than all the other facets which we have examined, and to this the Book of Job bears witness by ironically portraying the comfort of Job's friends as the heaviest part of his burden.

Up to now, our method of application, as we have been thinking of the various components of Job's problem, has been to put ourselves in his shoes, and see what we can learn both from his mistakes and from his triumph. To some extent we can do the same as we consider the way in which Job coped with his friends. But in the chapter on depression we have already had reason to cover the ground in this respect, since the failure of human sympathy is often, as in Job's case, an integral part of what it means to be depressed.

Here, however, are other shoes in which we may stand: not

Job's this time, as he looks with jaundiced eyes on the insipid offerings of his friends, but the shoes of the friends themselves. For the vicissitudes of life are such that we find ourselves cast at different times in different roles. Sometimes we are in Job's position, needing to receive counsel, but at other times we are called upon to be Job's comforters. It is to lessons for this latter task that we turn now.

It will be best to begin the enquiry with a word about the way in which the book as a whole provides a charter for the true pastor. This may be understood if we consider first a doctor's position. A doctor can, of course, combine his role with that of a spiritual adviser. But apart from this he is fighting what in the nature of things is bound to be a losing battle. Indeed, for a non-Christian doctor this must be, if he allows himself to think about it, a source of gnawing frustration. A Christian doctor can make sense of his profession as being essentially the performance of an acted parable (and this—as needs saying today in churches overcharged with excitement about bodily healing—is the most illuminating way of understanding Jesus' own work as a physician). In other words, bodily healing is an analogue of that wholeness which the human spirit desperately needs. Both are obtainable on earth. But while the former is limited to the extent that the human body is mortal and doomed to decay, it is a fading picture of something which is real, capable of increasing vitality (2 Cor. 3:18, 4:16), and carrying over to the life of heaven. For one who cannot look at medicine in this way, the inevitability of death poses an insoluble problem. But the Christian counsellor by contrast, is always in a position to offer a favourable prognosis. For, to put the matter in its baldest terms, to the unbeliever he can hold out the assurance that it is never too late to become a believer; and in the case of a believer, however dark may be the clouds of trouble or anxiety swirling about the head of the one whom he seeks to help, he knows that in the end they are bound to part, letting the sun of God's goodness and mercy shine through. This is not merely the message of Romans 8:28: it is the message of the Book of Job (cf. Jas. 5:11). For the final recovery of Job serves, as we have seen, to express the writer's conviction that when, to all appearances, everything is against the people of God and they go in the end to the wall, appearances are misleading. Somehow, sometime, God's faithfulness will turn out to restore them.

This perspective of hope Job's friends lacked. Their God was too small; and the most important qualification for pastoral work is to have a God the right size. As much as anything, the Book of Job is about the sovereign power and mercy of God. Therefore its message is one of vital relevance to anyone who speaks in the name of that God. Amos, Isaiah, Jeremiah and Ezekiel all experienced visions of the greatness of God before they began their ministry. And it was in the light of the understanding this experience afforded that they could face the worst, knowing that however unlikely it might seem, the God who was smiting could and would bind up; that though the end was coming, there was hope beyond the end. The ministry of the early church's most notable counsellor was similarly founded on his Damascus Road experience of power mingled with grace, and he was well aware that a true minister was nothing but a steward, a channel, an earthenware vessel, valuable only for the glory not his own which made him its vehicle. Paul was a small man with a great God, and all his virtues as a minister sprang from the space in his life filled by that God.

It is not too hard on Job's friends, on the other hand, to diagnose their failure in detail as but symptoms of this basic shortcoming: it led them to errors both in the realm of truth and in the realm of love.

1 Departure from truth

The friends made constant appeals to Job for repentance (11:13-14, 22:21, 35:14). At first they accused him of sin in a vague and general way, but in the end they did it quite specifically (22:5-9). As we have seen, their reason for doing this was their theological premiss that the tradition promised blessings to the righteous and misfortune to sinners. We have discussed above the basic fallacy in this position. But the crucial point here is that they made accusations about his behaviour for which there was no eye-witness evidence. And this was an error in the realm of truth, however much it may overspill into the realm of love.

Christians have often been guilty of this kind of mistake. It is a long time since Copernicus offended the church of his day by discovering the earth goes round the sun. But the lessons implicit in that controversy have taken too long to sink in. Even today there is a lingering tendency to regard the Bible as a scientific text-book in a way which is not consistent with its own fundamental distinction between the revelation of God in nature and the revelation of God in Scripture. This example may not too often affect counselling, though perhaps it is not uncommon for counsellors to be shunned precisely for obscurantism of this kind. But what does affect counselling without any doubt is when a theology founded precariously on a limited number of scriptural excerpts is brought to bear on a tricky pastoral situation. This inevitably leads to distorting the facts of the case, just as a garage mechanic with an inadequate range of spanners will spoil the nuts which do not match the ones he has, The counsellor turns into the frightful Procrustes of Greek mythology, who had two beds, one short and one long: his shorter guests were stretched till they fitted the longer bed, and his taller ones lopped till they fitted the shorter.

The remedy is clear enough. On the one hand, the counsellor must seek all the time to increase the breadth and depth of his biblical understanding. On the other, he must beware, when he is faced with awkward facts, of the temptation to square them with his current theological framework. Realization of the awkwardness is (as it should have been for Job's friends) a warning light driving one to a reassessment of the relevant biblical teaching. Job's friends ignored it. But they are there as a beacon for us. For we are all too good at jumping from the sight of a person's predicament to conclusions about the behaviour which we imagine must have brought it about.

It was something for which Job himself took his friends to task. What they had said, he objected, was lacking in tang:

> Can a man eat tasteless food unseasoned with salt,
> or find any flavour in the juice of mallows? (6:6).

Mallows (or purslane) were eaten as a salad vegetable, which needed seasoning to make it palatable. But there is more to it than that. Breaking the stem of the purslane plant causes it to exude a frothy liquid: the Arabs call it the 'idiot' plant for this reason. Job is not only saying that his friend's speech is insipid; he is making an even less complimentary insinuation. But the reference to salt is important enough to find an echo in Paul's letter to the Colossians: 'Let your speech always be gracious, seasoned with salt, so that you may know how you ought to answer every one' (Col. 4:6 RSV). We may gather from this that if our theology lacks freshness, if it degenerates into stereotyped, trite patterns, it is not a question of good theology served up badly, like a fine fried egg on a cold and dirty plate. It is not truly biblical theology at all. Salt cannot lose its savour. So if it has lost its savour, it cannot be salt, and Jesus said where it could go (Mt. 5:13). He himself is a model in this respect. He was utterly faithful to the Old Testament. But his presentation of its teaching, as for instance in the Sermon on the Mount, had a freshness which transfigured it. Masters of the art of spiritual counsel have always been characterized by this freshness: Augustine, Richard Baxter, Samuel Rutherford, Murray M'Cheyne, J. C. Ryle, to name but a few. But it needs to be done anew for every generation. Slavish imitation of past masters, as indeed *slavish* quotation of the text of Scripture will not suffice. The need is for the digestion of the Word of God by the counsellor—not its regurgitation. Jesus had so made Scripture part of himself that his teaching was distinctively his own and matched exactly the needs of his hearers. When this is done, there is a sharp contrast with the cold weight of tradition, which, as with Job's friends (5:27, 8:8) and the Scribes and Pharisees, is so near the letter, yet so far from the spirit of the truth.

2 Failures of love
Job's comforters are at least called friends (2:11, 32:3). And

to deserve it, let it be said in their defence, they did at least come. For seven days and nights they maintained a vigil which presents a challenge to any minister conscious that his own record of visiting is open to criticism as casual, rare, shallow or hurried. Job's brothers held aloof. His slave-girls treated him as a stranger. His kinsmen and intimates had slipped away. His retainers had forgotten him. He summoned his slave, but there was no reply (19:13-16). Yet these three friends were there.

It was sad that when they were such exceptions to the general abandonment of Job to his fate, they were not more helpful to him. We saw how they came with rigid theological preconceptions. But these were matched by others which trespassed more on sympathy than on truth. Their week-long watch, for a start, while it bore witness to their stamina, marked their judgement, as we considered earlier, that Job was more a candidate for mourning than counselling.[1] No wonder if Job's response to such treatment was to wish himself to the place where his friends had all but relegated him—or, better still, unborn.

The extent to which Job's friends are guilty of lacking sympathy depends in a measure on the interpretation of Eliphaz's opening speech. We have given reasons (pp. 47-8) for the view that his contribution from the start was bitingly ironical. If this is right, the friends' initial approach to Job appears on the scale of sympathy well below freezing point. The sympathetic counsellor is one who can put himself in the shoes of the one whom he seeks to help. For he knows how easily, but for the mysterious providence of God, he might actually be standing in them himself. Job's friends at no point give this impression. They view him from a detached vantage point, as though they were not made of the same flesh and blood at all. By contrast, the picture of Jesus is greatly heightened, as the high priest able to sympathize with our weaknesses because in his likeness to us he has been tested in every way (Heb. 4:15). His dying

---

[1] 'Seven days and nights', as a period of mourning, has parallels in Gen. 50:10, 1 Sam. 31:13, and, most important, Ecclesiasticus 22:12. But Pope cites the Babylonian Talmud, Moed Qatan 28b, to make the point that comforters were traditionally not permitted to speak until the mourner opened the conversation. If importance should be attached to this, the case against the friends here becomes more debatable.

love displays the costliness of involvement, and the parable of the Good Samaritan stands in the Gospel as a warning not to imagine that we have attained an adequate standard of sympathy. But before we can profit fully from the advanced lessons in this subject provided by Jesus' teaching and example, we do well to learn the elementary, if negative, lessons provided by Job's friends. Let us see the danger of insensitivity in Bildad's suggestion that Job's sons must have been great sinners (8:4) and the crassly inappropriate comment that if only Job would turn sincerely to God, then, though his beginnings had been humble, his end would be great (8:7). The reader has been prepared by the Prologue to pull a wry smile at this point. For he knows that Job went further than the second mile to protect his sons from misdemeanour (1:5); and as for his humble beginnings, he knows that Job was the greatest man in all the East (1:3). Yet for all their grossness, Bildad's mistakes are still being committed at hospital bedsides today.

An important summary of the friends' pastoralia is contained in the word of Elihu (32:17): 'I too have a furrow to plough'. The impression he gives is of the ploughman fixing his eye on the distant tree, and remorselessly churning up the ground at his feet without giving an inch to right or left. This is a tragically accurate portrait of Job's friends. Certainly there is a place for the preacher, who delivers his message without fear or favour, unbent by whatever hostility it may encounter. But this is not the right model for the counsellor. Job's friends saw faithfulness in terms of an uncompromising transmission of the truth as they had it in their minds deep-frozen and ready-packaged. Jehovah's Witnesses are reputed to be trained to do their door-to-door work in precisely this way, learning a set response for every dialectical versicle they are likely to come across. But it was not the way Jesus encouraged his own disciples to approach dialogue: they were to rely on words supplied by the Holy Spirit at the moment of encounter.

What this involves, of course, for the counsellor, is listening: and listening not only *to* what is actually spoken, but listening *for* the need which is clamant, as it were, between the lines. But this is precisely what Job's friends did not do. Certainly, they picked up some of Job's actual expressions and used them (unfairly) against him. But they had made a complete diagnosis before their conversation with him began; so they thought they had no need to listen, except for the purposes of collecting ammunition for their predetermined barrage. They insisted on carrying on the conversation along their own lines, and the result, unsurprisingly, was that to a large extent Job and his friends encountered each other like two trains, one on the up-track, and the other on the down, snorting past each other rather than actually meeting. Job was as much to blame as his friends. Yes. But Job was the case in this particular case-study. For him, inability to converse was simply a symptom commonly found in people suffering from depression: they become preoccupied with their own thoughts and their own way of looking at things; they become repetitive and lacking in concentration. But it is useless for the counsellor to give tit for tat. When we examine Jesus's skill as a pastoral conversationalist, particularly with the depressed Samaritan woman at Sychar[2] (Jn. 4:4 ff.), we find he made sparing use of assertion, and striking use of questions and requests. There are plenty of questions on the lips of Job's friends. But a glance at them is enough to show that they are almost entirely rhetorical. A question like Bildad's,

How long will you say such things,
the long-winded ramblings of an old man? (8:2)

is better calculated to shut the patient up than draw him out.

This leads us to a further mistake on the part of the friends: they were argumentative. Those who are depressed or in an acute state of anxiety tend to say wild things. Job was no exception. But it is no good reacting—as Job's friends did—antithetically, however tempting an attitude it might be to adopt. For such wild utterances often carry, implicitly or explicitly,

[2] For an unconscious comment on her depression by a modern psychiatrist, compare this excerpt from Ross Mitchell, *Depression*, Pelican 1975: 'Some depressed people rush into a hectic sexual life, going from one partner to another, hoping desperately to find that 'ideal' person who will meet all their needs, who will make them feel 100 per cent'.

an element of accusation or complaint. No doubt the counsellor does not think of himself as being in the place of God. But the one whom he is helping may well address him as though he were responsible for turning on and off all God's switches. An excellent example of this is the widow with whom Elijah stayed at Zarephath (I Kgs. 17:17 ff.). When her son stopped breathing, she turned on Elijah and said, 'What made you interfere, you man of God? You came here to bring my sins to light and kill my son!' It was not easy to do what Elijah did. Instead of retorting, 'How dare you accuse me of killing your son?' he bit his tongue—unlike Job's friends, who tumble headlong into this trap. 'What do you mean by treating us as cattle?' asks Bildad (18:3). And it is because he is riled that Eliphaz progresses from his initially veiled insinuations about Job's conduct to his outburst in 22:4–5:

> Do not think that he reproves you because you are pious,
> that on this count he brings you to trial.
> No: it is because you are a very wicked man.

The pastoral helper must never be riled. And what Elijah did when he stood on the edge of the precipice is instructive enough. 'Give me your son': he went to the heart of the woman's problem without becoming involved in a barren controversy about the extent of his own responsibility. Then, taking the boy's corpse upstairs, he called out, 'O Lord my God, is this thy care for the widow with whom I lodge?' Her complaint had been put into the wrong pigeon-hole; so he re-addresses it to its proper destination.

3 The generation gap

So far our discussion has been largely concerned with Job's relationship with Eliphaz, Bildad and Zophar. The contribution of Elihu merits separate treatment for two reasons. One is that his speeches constitute a quite distinct section in the book. But more important, the writer gives prominence to the point that Elihu is a younger man (32:6). We have already said something about the substance of the position which he represents (pp. 74 ff), and suggested that it may well be the writer's intention to make him the mouthpiece of a point of view which purported to be a new and definitive solution to the problem of suffering, but which the writer particularly disagreed with. The feasibility of this interpretation depends, as we saw, on regarding the Elihu section as an integral part of the book. Here we are going to be concerned with such lessons as may be learned from the personal interaction of Elihu with the other figures in the drama. But before we can make any headway, it will be as well to deal in more detail with the reasons for regarding this part of the book as genuine and original, since the argument here hangs on that premiss even more crucially.

A cursory comparison of the commentaries reveals an astonishing variety of opinions. These may be broadly divided into the two obvious groups: those who are for, and those who are against regarding the Elihu section as part of the original work. Critics who think it is a later addition tend to arrive at a low assessment of these chapters, though Dhorme regards Elihu as fulfilling a positive objective in spelling out (albeit beforehand) the detailed implications of the divine intervention. Those who think the Elihu section is part of the original are divided about whether he is to be regarded as the mouthpiece of the writer or not.

Two questions therefore emerge: (i) Is Elihu's contribution an authentic part of the book? (ii) Is it intended by the writer to be understood as the expression of his own view?

We begin by examining the arguments which have been used to prove that this section is a subsequent addition to the book. (*a*) *No explanation is given of Elihu's presence.* But the question why Elihu is not introduced at an earlier stage involves imposing canons of style on the work which may well be inapplicable; and in any case, the most this argument can prove is that Elihu's appearance represents a departure from the writer's initial plan. (*b*) *Neither Job, nor his friends, nor God takes any notice of Elihu.* But our thesis will be that their silence, which is certainly undeniable, has its own dramatic

point to make. In fact, God does endorse (without acknow-
ledgement) something that Eliuhu says, and this makes difficulties of its own for interpreting the section as the work of a
later writer proposing a wholly new solution. *(c) If Elihu anticipates God's final intervention, the climax is spoiled.* But this
would only be the case if no dramatically satisfying interpretation were possible, and as we shall see, it is far from obvious
that this is so. *(d) Style and language are different from the rest
of the book.* But the writer should be given credit for ability to
achieve this effect deliberately. If both the Prologue and the
bulk of the dialogue are his workmanship, such ability needs
no further demonstration. *(e) The poetry is of poorer quality.*
This argument might carry more weight if we did not find
many commentators claiming on the contrary that Elihu's contribution is poetically the best! However, the controversy on
this score may be the result of arguing at cross-purposes. The
solution here proposed is that while Elihu's couplets are very
finely chiselled, this is itself part of the artistry with which he
is discredited as polished, but pompous.

Two further points in favour of the section being part of the
original should be mentioned. The first is that Elihu takes no
account of the Prologue. This is difficult to reconcile with the
view that Elihu is the mouthpiece of a later interpolator's
'solution'. The second point brings us to the other of the
two questions posed above, concerning the extent to which the
writer intends to endorse what Elihu says. It is possible to
envisage a later interpolator introducing a new character to
voice his own entirely serious contribution. But four characteristics of what Elihu says discourage any such conclusion:
his anger, his pomposity, his long-windedness and above all the
fact that while he claims to shed new light on the dispute, most
of his points are anticipated by what Job's friends have already
said. Pope, it is true, claims that there would be no offence to
oriental ears in the way in which Elihu speaks,[3] and he argues
that the profuse introduction to the young man's speeches
should be seen as a fitting fanfare for the *pièce de resistance*.

[3] See above, p. 74.

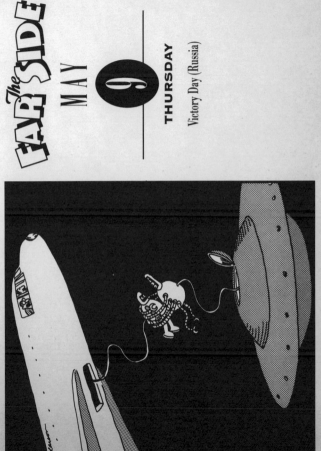

"We've done it! They've linked up! ... Man, Feldman must be freaking out—he even hates spiders."

But this view, quite apart from its intrinsic implausibility, does not by any means lead to a more integrated understanding of the book as a whole.

It would be wrong to regard Elihu as a cartoon character, and to exaggerate the extent to which he is mocked by the writer. As is true of all the participators in the discussion, Elihu too possesses a measure of the truth. Nevertheless, his main conclusion (one drawn earlier by Eliphaz) that Job's suffering is disciplinary is also the main theological error which the writer of the book in gunning against. That Elihu should sum up the friends' arguments in the manner of a judge is one of the writer's quiet jokes; but it serves his purpose well. Wearing, as it were, his college scarf and his debating society tie, Elihu is by far the most systematic of all the speakers in his presentation. The writer laughs at him, but at the same time the traditions of men are brilliantly marshalled for inspection before God descends in the whirlwind to blow upon them.

If this analysis is correct, it is legitimate to see Elihu as part of Job's problem, no less than his other friends. And quite apart from his theology, there are lessons to be learnt from his approach, and it seems appropriate to see these particularly in the light of his youth. Some of the lessons are obvious enough. We have seen how Elihu was patronizing, and the temptation to be patronizing is a very real one for young ministers and doctors. Closely linked with the over-familiarity, which stands as the clearest symptom of this in Elihu's case, is the way in which he gives the impression that the answer to Job's problem is easy and obvious, and pours scorn on Job's older counsellors for failing to produce the right advice. True, he affects to respect his elders, but the fact that it is merely an affectation only makes matters worse. His wordy introduction in chapter 32, far from being the prelude for the grand finale, seems much more like a tirade (from the writer) against bad manners and pompous verbosity. 'I too am only a handful of clay', says Elihu (33:6). But unlike Paul and Barnabas at Lystra (Acts 14:15) he was in no danger of being mistaken for a divine figure. The clear message for anyone who finds himself in the position of a counsellor as a young man or woman is: beware of self-importance.

There is another charge which must figure in our indictment of Elihu which is not unlike one which we levelled at the other friends, but which is accentuated by his youth. In 33:9–11, he quotes with undeniably literal accuracy Job's claim to innocence. But it is clear that Job had no intention of claiming sinless perfection (7:21, 13:26), and that the whole thrust of his defence lies in the plea that he is innocent of any charge which could adequately account for the sufferings which had befallen him. So Elihu is guilty of the policeman's trick of writing in his notebook that half of a defendant's statement which in its original context contributes reasonably to his excuse, but read by itself amounts to self-condemnation. To win a debating point like this may be slick, but higher standards of discussion are required from anyone acting in a pastoral capacity, with the aim not of winning some kind of game, but of helping a person. An elementary part of this is to make a fair appraisal of what the person says rather than to create an Aunt Sally out of some unrepresentative excerpt.

But what are we to say about the fact that Elihu says something which God himself endorses (37:14 ff.)? If, as we have argued, this cannot be allowed to count as a knock-down argument in favour of the writer's approval of Elihu, there is only one alternative: we must conclude that the message which sits comfortably enough in the mouth of God sits far from comfortably in the mouth of Elihu. What God says to Job with propriety may be most improper from this young man.

But the generation gap is not something for which only the young are responsible. While Elihu is implicitly, as the other friends are explicitly, the target of the writer's criticism, it is perhaps not unfair tentatively to make the point that there was no response to Elihu from Job or his other friends. There was no response from God either, but it is one thing for God to administer a rebuke in this way, and quite another for Elihu's elders to do so. His weakness was that he was tempted to see himself as God, as he pontificated on the whole affair. But for Job and his friends to behave towards him with divine disdain was ironically to fall into the same trap. It is all the more ironical, in that Elihu was telling Job, if he had patience to listen, at least something of what God himself was going to tell him. It may not be easy for older people to listen to what their juniors say, especially when the manner in which it is said leaves much to be justifiably desired. But it is the mark of wisdom to be prepared to accept light from any quarter. The young may have much to answer for in the creation of the generation gap. But nothing creates it more effectively than the refusal of those who are older to listen and communicate.

4 The true pastor

It is one of the subtle ironies of the Book of Job that though there were four candidates for the post of pastor, none of them was elected. Instead, at the end of the day, it was their sheep, so to speak, who was declared their shepherd. For the true pastor in the Book of Job was none other than Job himself. What qualifications did he have to justify this decision on the part of God?

The evidence is contained partly in the Prologue, where Job's pastoral concern for his family (1:5) reflects the shepherdly care exercised (as Satan complains) by God over him (1:10). That good shepherds are those who know a Good Shepherd is a truth writ large all over the face of Scripture, most clearly in the career of David, though paradoxically not so much by his positive example (2 Sam. 9:5, 23:17), as by the arguments used by Nathan to bring him to his senses on the occasion of his greatest lapse (2 Sam. 12:1–14). God's shepherdly care, unlike that of the greatest human exponent short of Jesus himself (Jn. 10) is never relaxed. There is exquisite irony in Job's complaint that it is the lot of mankind to have their way hedged in by God (3:23), when this has been the precise expression of Satan (1:10), objecting to God's vigilant protection of Job.

Then, secondly, we have the sarcastic words of Eliphaz (4:3–4). Just as there is no more telling evidence that Jesus did actually perform miracles than that his opponents were driven to explaining them as being done by the power of

Beelzebul, so here we find that Job's friend could not open his mouth without coming to grips with the sufferer's outstanding reputation as a pastor:

Think how once you encouraged those who faltered,
how you braced feeble arms,
how a word from you upheld the stumblers
and put strength into weak knees.

It makes no difference for our purpose here whether sarcasm is the right construction to put upon these words. In any case, they provide a sufficiently telling picture of Job's pastoral qualities: the words are an echo of Isa. 35:3, which is quoted as a precept without amendment by the writer to the Hebrews (12:12).

Thirdly, there are the claims made by Job in his own self-defence, together with the complaints that he made about his friends. From the former, we gain material for expanding the brief tribute of Eliphaz (31:16–20). From the latter, we can infer how Job would have behaved if the roles had been reversed. At least he would have been sympathetic rather than haranguing his clients (16:4–5). At least he would have listened instead of making unjust accusations (21:2). Above all, he would have been aware of the worst shortcoming of all, that there should be those who look to one for pastoral help, as a desert traveller looks to the distant *wadi* for water, but go away disappointed, with thirst unquenched (6:20, 21).

Finally, there is God's own certificate of worthiness. Here is the linchpin of the whole argument. The one who has all the time seemed to be the person in need of help is the one whom God declares to be qualified to help those who have failed to help him. One is reminded of the turning of the tables when the risen Christ appears to the Peter who has signally failed to stand by his master (Jn. 21:15 ff.). For those who gave him no succour at the hour of his trial he 'ever liveth to make intercession'. To those who gave him vinegar to drink he has opened a fountain of living water. Job was qualified as a pastor before his trial, but much more by it. For the supreme qualification is to be one for whom the personal bond with God comes first, and Job has been proved to be a man of this kind. It is some comfort to those who emulate his pastoral role that all this was in spite of great mistakes: some he made himself; many more were made by his friends. Through the most meaningless experience and the cathartic process of reacting to the most imperfect counsellors, Job was equipped as a minister. And the ministry for which he was qualified was a ministry of prayer. There are many shepherdly things which Christian friends can do for one another, but none of them is more important or far-reaching than intercession. For while God condescends to use our hands to fulfil his purposes, prayer makes it possible to use his.

PART TWO: — GOD'S ANSWER

1 The essence of wisdom

It was out of a whirlwind that God at last spoke to Job. This in itself was no accident, for a whirlwind was a fitting symbol of both the points which God was at pains to make in his two-part sermon. Of uncertain origin and destination, the whirlwind reminds man of his limited grasp of the natural world—Jesus was one day to stress this truth to Nicodemus (Jn. 3:8); on the other hand, its certain power points to the even more certain power of its own creator and controlling hand.

Where was Job when the world was made? The first aim of God's speech is to show how limited Job is, both in time and space. Just as he cannot probe from the confines of a life lived late in time to the day when first the morning stars sang together (38:7), so neither can he probe in space the springs of the sea (38:16) or the storehouse of the snow, the arsenal where hail is stored (38:22).

Clearly, Job is to learn that the world is a miracle of efficiency, and at the same time full of questions which he cannot begin to answer. Yet this was the man presuming to teach God his business and to make comments about the way the world was governed. Was he wise to do this?

Job acknowledges that he had better say no more (40:3–5). But there was more to come from God. One of the implications of Job's criticisms was that if God knew what it was right to do, and of this truth he remained convinced, then he must lack the power to do it. Probably, the animal described in God's second onslaught is the crocodile, as the New English Bible concludes (40:15). But when we find firebrands shooting from his mouth, and sparks streaming out, it is clear that the description is being carried through in a style which owes much to stories of dragons. Such stories abounded in the Near East, particularly in myths about creation. In the biblical account of creation there is striking avoidance of any mention of such monsters, but there are figurative references to them, sometimes applying to Egypt, in the Old Testament: for instance, Rahab (Ps. 89:10), and Leviathan (Ps. 74:13 f.). It would be a mistake then to think that God is basing his claims to power here on the creation of the common or garden crocodile: the crocodile is metamorphosed as a symbol of all the forces of chaos and evil which God has subdued. It is in the light of this that Job is challenged to decide whether he has been wise to speak as he has.

Viewed like this, the answer of God to Job is a simple one. But it is very important to recognize that the exact nuance of the divine contribution depends on all that precedes it. To take it out of its context, as though this were the whole message and could stand alone, is to distort its real meaning. The whole book may be viewed as an essay on true wisdom, and in the deepest sense it is the whole book which must be regarded as God's answer to Job. To see this perspective is the object of this chapter. It involves asking to what extent Job himself was wise, and to what extent his friends were lacking in wisdom; and means also examining the relationship between the interaction of Job with his friends and his encounter with God at the end, in the complex process by which the total divine answer was communicated to him.

We saw earlier how the very first verse of the book confronts us with the question of Job's righteousness. But it also confronts us with the question of his wisdom. Not only do we read that Job was a man of upright life, but that he feared God. This statement is certainly equivalent to a claim that he was wise. The book is full of raging controversy, but at one point there is a large measure of agreement between Job and his friends throughout the dialogue: that the fear of the Lord is the beginning of wisdom (Ps. 111:10). The implications of the first verse of the Book of Job are brought out clearly by the proverb which speaks to the same effect:

> Do not think how wise you are,
> but fear the Lord and turn from evil (Prov. 3:7).

The Prologue contains further evidence that Job was wise. 'The Lord gives and the Lord takes away', says Job in the teeth of calamity (1:21). And this is glossed by the writer, 'He did not charge God with folly'. Not to charge God with lack of wisdom is clearly regarded as the mark of man's not lacking it either. The same point is made again when Job's wife advises him to curse God: this is the policy of a foolish woman, and the writer expresses approval of Job's attitude in words very similar to those which he had used before (1:22, 2:10).

But just as the dialogue introduces us to complications in the question whether Job was righteous, so it does too in the question whether he was wise. It is clear enough that Job's friends are being criticized for their style of wisdom. But the criticism is subtle. Much of what they say appears to have scriptural backing. Some of it agrees with what God himself says in the book. And what is more, while the writer largely sympathizes with Job, particularly in his attacks on the pretentiousness of his comforters, Job himself does not maintain a perfectly wise course throughout the debate.

Let us begin by probing what the book as a whole teaches as the essence of wisdom. In the Prologue, Job's wisdom consists in refusing to deny wisdom to God. But what can we learn about God's wisdom? Again and again, in one way and another, God's wisdom is connected with his creative activity. As elsewhere in the Bible, God's activity as creator is linked closely to his government of the universe. God's rebuke at the end of the book makes this point: the limitations of Job's wisdom consist in his failure to recognize throughout the dialogue (in spite of his noble words in the Prologue) the unlimited extent of God's wisdom. The root of Job's misgivings about God is this: if God knew all (and Job does not dispute this), he would see that his sufferings were utterly inappropriate. God's answer is that, on the contrary, if Job knew all (and the reader is given an insight by the Prologue as to what this might mean), he would see that his sufferings were serving to vindicate the profound personal character of the relationship between God and a godly man.

Of course God does not reveal to Job what the reader learns

in the Prologue. Had he done so, the book would have lost much of its value for anybody in a comparable position to Job's. Suffering elicits from us an agonizing 'Why?' But experientially we never know why at the moment of suffering. And the Book of Job does not so much comfort us with the thought that there is a tidy, rational explanation which, if only we knew it, would entirely satisfy us and remove the sting. Rather it challenges the sufferer to maintain his trust in the competence and love of God in an area where he is tempted to doubt it—on the strength of God's undeniable competence in areas where man only has to open his eyes to reassure himself. What we see when we open our eyes is God's creative power. And this, so God argues, should bring home to us how fragmentary and inadequate our understanding is.

But then the problem arises, is this not what the friends themselves were trying to din into Job? Does not Eliphaz, for instance, make precisely this point when he says,

> For my part, I would make my petition to God
> and lay my cause before him,
> who does great and unsearchable things,
> marvels without number.
> He gives rain to the earth . . . 5 : 8–10).

What is this but seeking to persuade Job to trust God on the basis of his creative power? And yet we know that the writer does not want us to see Eliphaz as the pillar of wisdom he imagines himself to be.

1 Why are Job's friends not truly wise?
The answer summarily is that although Eliphaz says things which, taken by themselves, are in harmony with the writer's own outlook, other things that he says alter the character of such passages, and show them to be part of an entirely different perspective.

The friends, first of all, are shameless utilitarians. Repentance, in the estimation of Eliphaz, is a kind of insurance policy. Making petition to God is advocated, not for the intrinsic value of a relationship with him, but simply for the pay-off in material terms—as when he says,

Come to terms with God and you will prosper;
that is the way to mend your fortune (22:21).

The interesting point here is that the friends adopt precisely the position which Satan regards as universally occupied by those who make a show of being god-fearing. 'Does Job fear God for nothing?' he had asked. And whatever the answer to his question, Eliphaz makes no secret of the grounds on which he is advising Job to fear God. It is all too shallow. Faith is de-personalized: it becomes self-centred instead of God-centred. Its character as faith is destroyed. Fear of God is simply not the right way to describe it.

A true view of God's creative power produces the psalmist's reaction, 'What is man that thou art mindful of him?' (Ps. 8:4). It gives one a proper estimate of God and oneself. But Eliphaz's outlook is still man-centred in spite of all he says about creation. God's power is simply something to be taken into account, something to be manipulated by appropriate, outwardly law-abiding behaviour, in the same impersonal way that fourth-formers look at schoolmasters, not as people, but as obstacles to be negotiated.

This way of looking at God leads precisely to that distortion of the facts which provides Job with the grounds for his bit-terest complaint about his friends—and ultimately for God's own indictment. Job forecasts that God will not be pleased with their false advocacy (13:10), and this turns out to be an accurate prophecy. But their world-view demanded this blink-ered analysis. There had to be a predictable correspondence between 'righteousness' and prosperity, 'wickedness' and mis-fortune, simply because their relationship with God was not deep enough to make any other kind of security possible.

The friends were buoyed up by their claim that it was the tradition of the elders that they were purveying. Bildad re-commends Job to make enquiry of older generations and con-sider the experience of their fathers: 'Will not they speak to

you and teach you and pour out the wisdom of their hearts?'
(8:8, 10). 'We are mere creatures of yesterday and are tran-
sient', he insists in the same context. With less modesty, Eliphaz
purports not so much to point to tradition as to embody it
with his own avuncular white hair (15:10). But in any case
the parallels to the book in older pagan literature bear out the
friends' claim to be mouthpieces of the centuries-old wisdom
of the Near East. To this extent the Book of Job is indeed the
child of a literary tradition which arose in a cosmopolitan
milieu of remote antiquity. What is distinctive about our
writer, however, is that he does not endorse the 'wisdom' of
Bildad and Eliphaz. Certainly his book reflects the time-
honoured ideas of what wisdom consists of. But his objective
is to criticize them.

The point of his criticism is perfectly plain. After Zophar's
patronizing rebuke in Chapter 11, implying that a suitable dose
of divine wisdom would soon reduce Job to silence, Job begins
his reply with an ironical eulogy of his friends' supposed wisdom. Their 'wisdom' is bogus for the simple reason that it
leads them to ignore evidence which is as plain as a pikestaff
to the brute beasts (12:7 f.)—namely that what prevails in the
world is the law of the jungle.

Who cannot learn from all these
that the Lord's own hand has done this? (12:9)

looks like a sarcastic protest against too simplistic an understanding of Is. 41:20b, where the prophet is speaking not
about the chaos but the order in the universe. But in the succeeding verses, we must be careful to allow for hyperbole in
what Job goes on to say. He is not in all seriousness insisting,
as appears on the face of it, that the whole gamut of God's
activity is uniformly perverse. He purposely exaggerates the
problem of understanding God's government of the world in
order to wake his friends up to the fact that there is a problem
to be wrestled with, that it simply will not do to take the line,
'God's in his heaven and all's right with the world'.

Job significantly turns the tables on his friends here. They accuse him of having no fear of God because of the way he is speaking; and having no fear of God, as we have seen, is synonymous with folly. Job, however, replies to this by proving that they too show their lack of fear for God. Otherwise they would not insult him by wilful blindness to the plain facts of their experience. God would not be impressed by such intellectual dishonesty.

There is also another side to the friends' theology which needs to be noticed. If what we have been looking at can be called the mercenary or utilitarian aspect of their view of God, we must now examine the fatalistic aspect. Eliphaz (5:17–27), Bildad (8:6–7), and Zophar (11:14 ff.) all promise Job God's future blessing if he will but change his attitude. But one look at the disease-ridden, worm-eaten Job must have been enough to make the prospect of the kind of restoration they envisaged somewhat remote. And so we find a less optimistic version of the same basic philosophy.

The reason why it is still the same basic philosophy is that it is still founded on a concept of God as impersonal power. Channel it, if you can, they say in effect, to your own advantage by conformist behaviour. But if it proves impossible, it is no use arguing. God is an imperial dictator with innumerable squadrons of troops, able to pounce out of ambush-positions all the way along the unfortunate traveller's road (25:3 f.). This is Bildad's final word of comfort to Job, and it has a strangely modern ring about it, echoed as it is by the pessimism of much recent fiction and philosophy. In the same vein, Elihu, after repeating Eliphaz's argument that God is not personally interested in human behaviour (cf. 22:3 and 35:7), ends up by implying that one might as well argue with a thunderstorm as with God (37:20–4).

It is worth considering that the degeneration of faith into utilitarianism or fatalism is not something peculiar to Eliphaz and his colleagues. The New Testament has much to say of the mercenary characteristics of the Scribes and Pharisees, and the tacit equation of wealth with godliness and divine approval was a popular fallacy which Jesus himself took care to nail in the discussion with his disciples (Lk. 18:28–30) after the encounter with the rich young ruler. But it was not Scribes and Pharisees who were expected to read the documents which later became the New Testament. It is Christians who must learn from their mistakes.

Today, there are two ways in which the teaching here invites application. The first concerns the way in which Christianity has very often brought with it a rise in living standards. This is obvious in Africa at the present time, as it was obvious in England in the experience of the early Methodists. And it is obvious not only to disinterested social historians, but to those among whom the changes are taking place. In India, the term 'rice-Christian' has arisen to describe those who profess the faith simply to better themselves materially. In our society the temptation takes subtler forms. But the fact that the Church is predominantly middle-class is a warning of the danger that exists of our using Christianity as a mere tool for obtaining prestige or material objectives. And whether succumbing to this temptation takes the form of snobbery or social climbing, it is closely related to the utilitarianism which characterized Job's friends.

The second point concerns a notable cleavage in the Church of our day. On the one hand, there are those with avowed left-wing sympathies, who at their most extreme would be prepared to give support to armed revolutionary movements in South Africa and elsewhere, and at the end of the day might not frown on the unconstitutional overthrow of the capitalist economy of the West. On the other hand, there are those who equate Christianity with opposition to such a stance, and with the upholding (not always by the fairest means) of the political *status quo*. It is such people who are guilty of a kind of utilitarianism, inasmuch as there is often a selfish insensitivity to Third-World needs latent in their position.

This division is reflected with great accuracy in the situation with which Jesus was confronted. On the left, there were the Zealots who advocated violent and unconstitutional measures to bring about radical change in society. On the right, there were the Herodians who were blindly in favour of things as they were. They could see the milk and honey of Roman rule, and they were indifferent to the injustices which went along with it, and on which it depended.

Now Jesus was no Zealot. From the Temptations (particularly the one which took him to the top of the high mountain and promised him wide dominion in return for worshipping Satan) and much else in the Gospel-story culminating in the popular disappointment of Palm Sunday, it is clear how he had to be constantly on his guard against this kind of simplistic political solution. But the point to be noticed here is this. If Jesus was no Zealot, neither was he an Herodian. For Jesus, Herod was 'that fox'. What this means is that, if the kind of 'zealotry' described above should be criticized from a biblical standpoint, those who engage in such criticism must be careful not to fall into the opposite error. For that opposite error is simply in modern guise the utilitarianism of Job's friends.

Fatalism is less easy to find in the New Testament. But something like it is seen in Thomas, at the point when Jesus determines to go to Jerusalem. 'Let us also go, that we may die with him', he says, in tones of abject pessimism. For him the cross which he anticipated was anything but an instrument for triumphantly achieving liberty, as Paul later placarded it. It was the inevitable blank wall at the end of the fruitless journey. But because of the way in which Christians understand the blank wall of the cross to have been transformed into a door by Jesus's resurrection (as Thomas himself came to understand), they of all people should be the least fatalistic. Yet it is not uncommon to find professing Christians who are pessimistic in their general outlook—for whom God is exactly, in practice, the omnipotent dictator with crushing hostile armies, the inexorable overwhelming thunderstorm: for to see the way they behave in face of life, this is what one would think they were up against.

2 Job's wisdom and its limitations

The great thing about Job was that he did not fall into either of these traps. His own experience, no doubt, was enough to cure him of thinking that godliness was in any easy sense equivalent to well-being. It was certainly his realism, however he came by it, for which God commended him at the end. The other aspect is more important because it speaks more loudly of the personal quality of Job's faith. Throughout his misery, and whatever he may have said amiss, Job was insistent on discovering God. 'O that I knew where I might find him', he cries (23:3). Even when he felt overwhelmed by the bitterness of his suffering, he was garrisoned by the certainty that behind it all stood a person—a person whom he knew, a person who certainly had become mysterious and incomprehensible, a person against whom he let fly a barrage of complaints, but in the end a person. If God became impersonal, it was not something which he could submissively accept. It was because he never lost hold of God as a person that Job could never be called a fatalist. And negatively we may say that it was in the avoidance of utilitarianism and fatalism that Job's wisdom lay. What this means positively is that he showed an inextinguishable respect for God as a person, even in his most violent complaints. So there was a sense in which Job at no point wholly abandoned that fear of the Lord which is the beginning of wisdom.

But while it may be argued that this analysis does justice to the skeleton of the book, there are some important areas which it leaves for further discussion.

First, it has to be admitted that there is an element of paradox in our contention that Job's wisdom was not submerged in the course of his dialogue with the friends. If, after all, we want to point to his restraint in the Prologue as evidence for his wisdom, are we not bound by the same token to see his wild outbursts later on as evidence for his folly? And if this is not so, must there not be somewhere something in the book which does not add up? It is, of course, arguments of this kind which lead many critics to regard the Book of Job as composite: between the Prologue and dialogue, they say, there is indeed a discrepancy in the portrait of Job which cannot be explained without resort to a theory of diversity of authorship. But the view taken here is that this conclusion raises more problems than it solves, and that a solution in terms of unity

of authorship and purpose does not involve anything out-
landish. There is no psychological unlikelihood in Job's beginning by submissively accepting his troubles, but then being
riled into bitter indignation by the unhelpfulness of his friends.
One is not obliged to interpret his initial resignation as fatalism,
since not all resignation is fatalistic (though some may be). Nor
is one obliged to defend his subsequent outbursts as reflections
of Job's underlying wisdom, though we have given reasons for
refusing to see them as absolutely contradicting the thesis that
Job was wise. Indeed the two propositions with which one has
to reckon are (i) that Job was rebuked by God for things which
he had said in the dialogue, but (ii) that he was also praised by
God for being fairer to him in what he said than his friends
had been. The conclusion is clear: there is built into the book
in a way which cannot possibly be ironed out an element of
inconsistency between a Job who in his underlying character
was a man of very great wisdom, and a Job who under severe
testing departed *in a measure* from the principles which that
same wisdom would have taught him.

If this prompts the reply, 'Can Job be both wise and un-
wise?' the answer may be to point to the biblical gallery of
God's heroes. Is there one of them, apart from Jesus himself,
who does not present us with a similar dilemma? There is a
particularly close parallel with Moses. Enjoying the distinction
of being the meekest man in all the earth (Num. 12:3), he
nevertheless betrayed himself on a crucial occasion with an
action which was anything but meek, and excluded himself
from the privilege of entering the promised land (Num. 20:12).

The exact thrust of God's rebuke to Job is something which
we have already had to discuss in dealing with the question
whether Job was righteous. His mistake lay in criticizing God's
style of government. Though he had in effect berated his friends
for playing God in their approach to him, he himself had been
guilty of the same thing by crediting himself with sufficient
wisdom to say what God should do.

This brings us to the second problem: how is chapter 28 to
be interpreted? Some answer must be given to this question in
any treatment of wisdom in the Book of Job. There are those

who rate the poetry of this chapter as the high-point of the whole work, and certainly wisdom is its central theme. The difficulty is this. Does the chapter belong to the original dialogue? Was it intended as a kind of interlude (rather like the contributions by the chorus in a Greek drama)? Or was it an extraneous poem included by a later editor, who regarded its theme as relevant to the Book of Job?

To discuss these issues in detail is beyond the scope of this book, but the view we take is that two points deserve emphasis in resolving the problem. One is that there is no textual evidence for not regarding Job as the speaker. The other is that the admittedly self-contained character of the chapter and its lack of clear connecting links with what precedes and what follows do not necessarily mark the passage as an intrusion, however delightful, from outside the unity of the work as a whole. This kind of argument involves imposing canons of style, which, as we have elsewhere had to notice, we have no right to do.[1]

At the very least, therefore, an attempt to interpret the chapter as an utterance of Job needs no apology. But it does raise an admittedly troublesome question. First of all, it is hard to imagine the passage as reflecting anything except the writer's conviction. But if Job is credited with such a statement, couched as it is in winsomely attractive terms, does this not make the end of the book a complete anti-climax? For at this rate, Job is brought to see the error of his ways before the divine harangue begins, it seems; yet this conclusion is plainly unthinkable.

The most hopeful solution is this. Job has been rebuking his friends for their assumed omniscience and for their over-confident analysis of his predicament. The end of chapter 27 is bitterly ironical (unless the text is faulty and a lost speech of Zophar is to be reconstructed here). But Chapter 28 is too

[1] The dangers are illustrated by the assertion at one time confidently made that the Book of Job made no secret of the manner of its composition (since it was written partly in prose and partly in verse). But then an Egyptian work of the second millenium BC was discovered, even somewhat similar in subject matter to the Book of Job: this too has a prose prologue and epilogue with a centrepiece in verse. See John A. Wilson tr. 'The Protests of an eloquent peasant', in J. B. Pritchard (ed.) *Ancient Near Eastern Texts relating to the Old Testament*, Princeton University Press (3rd edition 1969), pp. 407–10.

lyrical to be construed as continued irony. And while Job is continuing to rebuke his friends, it is now in a much quieter and more reflective vein.

The message of the poem is plain. It begins with a description of mining operations and sees these as an illustration of human ability to explore areas of the earth withheld from any other living thing, and to bring up hidden treasures by his technological ingenuity. When the poem originated, mining was perhaps equivalent in its novelty and impressiveness, to space travel and bringing back rocks from the moon. This suggests that it is wrong to denigrate modern technology, as some Christians are tempted to do, but entirely legitimate to point the same wistful contrast: man's competence is so formidable in many areas of his life; and yet when it comes to the basic questions, his attempts to find his own answers are doomed to pathetic failure.

> [Man] brings the hidden riches of the earth to light.
> But where can wisdom be found? (11–12).

It cannot be found anywhere (13–14). It cannot be purchased (15–19). God alone knows the answer, and this is his wisdom. Man's wisdom, on the other hand, lies in respectful recognition of his limitations and in a dependence on God which is reflected in moral integrity (28:28).[2]

Now if it is right to ascribe chapter 28 to Job (as the text does), Job is here preaching to his friends. It is they who have laid claim to wisdom, speaking as though Job's theological problems were easy to resolve, and as though it were easy to advise him what to do. Job is recommending a less opinionated

---

[2] It may be felt that one difficulty in the way of this interpretation of chapter 28 lies in this last verse. Job's recommendation of moral goodness at this point may seem too far a cry from his earlier cynicism (ch. 21) and irony (ch. 27) to be dramatically intelligible. One way of resolving this is to regard verse 28 as a later gloss. The use of the word for 'Lord' is without parallel in the rest of the book, and the phrase, 'And he said to man' does not fit into the poetic scheme (see Dhorme, op. cit., p. 414, Pope, op. cit., p. 183).

approach to God in the light of what he understands to be the true position of man's limited knowledge.

3 God's wisdom

But this paves the way for us to understand God's final intervention. The message which Job has been impressing on his friends God now proceeds to impress upon him. He has accused them, in effect, of laying claim to a kind of knowledge which they did not, and could not as human beings possess. Now God turns the same argument much more fiercely on Job himself. He is guilty of making the same mistake. True, he does not misrepresent any facts (as they all too cruelly do). But he counts without the backcloth to the facts—against which, as the reader knows, their significance is entirely different.

We are now in a position to draw together the message of the Book of Job in so far as it is a book about wisdom. The writer has two errors in mind which he is seeking to correct. One is the inadequacy of applying the message of Deuteronomy too rigidly to the case of an individual, an error very much akin to the Pharisaism of the New Testament, with its tendency to selfish utilitarianism or despairing fatalism. The other we can understand in the light of Israel's history. No doubt the nation's sufferings were sufficiently explained as the punishment for a corrupt establishment. To put it bluntly, the Jews, *as a nation*, deserved the catastrophe of the exile. But what was a righteous individual to make of it all? The message of our writer, intelligible enough in such a context (and intelligible too to many a twentieth-century believer caught up involuntarily in an alien political maelstrom) is that the moment of despair has not come. If we but knew the unrevealed secrets of God, we should see that there is an answer to undeserved suffering: an answer to the question why it begins, and why it can be so severe, and an answer in terms of ultimate compensation. More important still, the writer wants to impress upon his readers that human wisdom in such a situation consists in refusal to lose faith in a God who is all-wise.

It is impossible at this point not to relate the thought of the Book of Job to the Christian revelation. The cross of Jesus is

God's wisdom. Like all undeserved suffering (of which it is indeed the cardinal example), it too can be explained in terms of the purpose of God. There is, of course, one crucial contrast between the sufferings of Jesus and the sufferings of Job. Jesus deliberately set his face to go to Jerusalem with all that he knew it to entail. The New Testament emphasises the clarity with which he anticipated both the horror and the ultimate outcome of what lay ahead. Job, on the other hand, had no inkling of the trouble which was coming to him until its unheralded onset. Nor had he any understanding of its purpose in the intentions of God while it was actually in progress. But while allowances must be made for this contrast, there are at the same time profound similarities between the two situations. Not only does Jesus's willing death mark the vindication of the relationship between him and his father in heaven, but it is also redemptive—the merest hint of such a plan comes seminally in Job's intercession for his friends. On the other hand (also like Job's suffering), the cross can be explained in terms of the compensation which made it worthwhile. The reason why the Greeks thought that the cross was foolishness (I Cor. 1:18–24) lies partly in the sophisticated reaction of mockery at the preaching of the resurrection (cf. Acts 17:32). It was for the joy that was set before him that Jesus endured the cross. And it was this that made 'wisdom' an intelligible word to describe what might otherwise have been an act of meaningless, fruitless self-denial.

The Prologue and the Epilogue of the Book of Job hold the key to two questions to which Job did not know the answers. One was 'What is the explanation of this trouble?' and the other was 'What will make up for this trouble and put an end to it?' In some ways the Christian can find an answer to both of these questions in what he knows of Christ. He has no need to speculate about the redemptive purpose of God and the part that a believer's suffering can play in its achievement. Nor is there need to look to a mere symbol of vindication and restoration in the way that the latter days of Job were a symbol for the writer of some reversal, sometime, somehow, to make sense of this world's frustrations. The resurrection of Jesus *is* the reversal. And faith in the risen Jesus means that heaven begins now for those who through him become sons of God (I Jn. 5:11–13).

But this is not all that there is to be said. It can still be a secret shrouded in thick darkness why a particular Christian is singled out for a particular tribulation. And whatever delight in the foretaste of heaven the spirit of Christ affords us now, 'it doth not yet appear what we shall be' (I Jn. 3:2 AV). Only beyond shall we know as we are known (I Cor. 13:12). So though there is a sense in which Christ provides an answer to Job, there is also a sense in which, kept in the dark as he was, Job is still the model for every believer. And the wisdom he learnt is the wisdom we must learn from him.

2 Restoration

God's answer to Job is expressed not only in argument, but in action. After the severity of the sermon, there is an element of surprise in his being awarded the gold medal of divine approval, coined no longer in mere words, but in complete rehabilitation.

For some, this happy ending spoils the book. We emerge, it seems to them, from the savage, yet magnificent realism of the poem's centrepiece into the cloudless sky of sheer fantasy, and this, they object, is not how human stories end in real life.

There may be those who choose to approach this kind of objection with the claim that at least in this case there was a happy ending, insisting on the historically factual character of the book. But while there is no need to be too sceptical about a foundation in history for the story of Job, firmer ground exists to be defended in the thesis that there is a historical situation more important for our writer than the patriarchal days of his hero. For the portrait of Job is painted, as we have seen, in colours which the writer found on the palette of Jewish experience in the sixth century. We do not know whether the book was written immediately after the return from exile, or (what seems more likely) at a somewhat later period, when it was realized that the return had not, to put it mildly, solved all the problems of God's people. But the book stands as a profession of faith that there is in the plan of God a happy outcome for his people, and not only for them, but also for the individual believer. Certainly, this profession of faith is rooted in history, but it is the history of God's restoration of his suffering people which is important as history. The writer is using that solid factual datum to translate into individual terms the message of his people's career.

The happy ending of the Book of Job thus takes its place along with much else in the detail of the Bible, and with its overall plan when looked at as a whole, as evidence that the philosophical view of life which is so fashionable today is wrong: or at least it is an outlook which cannot be reconciled with that of the biblical writers. The idea that travelling hopefully is an adequate substitute for arriving, or the best substitute available when arriving is out of the question, obviously cannot be squared with what Paul says about resurrection in I Corinthians 15, and it cannot be squared with the Book of Job either. It is not surprising in a day when the attempt is made to subtract from Christianity the reality of rising from the dead that we find parallel enthusiasm for subtracting the Epilogue from the Book of Job, or explaining it away (as we have seen[1]) as though the writer must be joking!

These introductory remarks remind us that there are three phases which can be distinguished in approaching the task of interpreting Job's restoration. One can look at it in terms of the Old Testament writer's intentions, which is the fundamental method of exegesis. One can look at it, secondly, in terms of the place occupied by the Book of Job in the Bible as a whole, which involves a forward look into the New Testament just as the first method involves a backward look into the Old. And, finally, one can look at it in the light of our present situation.

1 The writer's intentions

Job was not without sin, and he was not without folly. Yet the Epilogue marks the vindication of a man who was fundamentally both righteous and wise. In comparison with the literature on which the writer draws most heavily (the Prophets and Psalms), a striking feature of the story of Job is that its hero is both an individual and a Gentile. In the teaching of Jeremiah and Ezekiel we find emerging in the Old Testament a much more explicit concern for the faith of the individual, just as in the later parts of Isaiah, and in the books of Ruth and Jonah, there is spelt out a conviction that the God of Israel is a God for everyman. The Book of Job must be seen as the endorsement of both these insights. That is, the hope

[1] See p. 76 above.

which it holds out is a hope which transcends the racial confines of Israel, and refuses to be content with a concept of individual fulfilment limited (like the promise to Abraham, so long as this is interpreted literally) to the destiny of a race.

But in any emphasis on Job as an individual there is a danger of losing a most important feature of the Epilogue. His exodus was not only an exodus for him. It was an exodus for his friends. Part of the irony of the whole drama is that from a spiritual point of view they were in a much worse case, just as Job was in a much better case than any *prima facie* appraisal might suggest. It was only after his prayer that Job was restored. His restoration was bound up with what we may perhaps call the conversion of his friends.

This combination of vicarious suffering and intercession has a complex history in the Old Testament. Something like it is seen in Abraham, whose prayer for Lot must have been an advanced lesson in spirituality for those who remembered that Lot was the father of the Moabites. Moses provides a much closer parallel, since on his shoulders, through his prayers and at his expense, the Israelites finally penetrated the promised land. But the passage which has the closest affinities with the Book of Job is Isaiah 52:13–53:12. For much is made there of the fact that the servant intercedes for the transgressors, and that the combination of his suffering and his prayer has a resuscitating effect upon them spiritually, reflected in the restoration which he himself is promised. It may be that the prophet is himself going beyond the idea of what the sufferings of Israel as a nation might achieve to a picture of an individual redeemer. If so, the bonds between this passage and Job are even closer—the last word on its interpretation has scarcely yet been spoken. Whether or not this is so, however, it seems clear that the writer of Job is going beyond a message merely applicable to Israel. He is surely saying something much more general about the opportunities opened up by the sufferings of a godly man—how they can, in conjunction with his prayers, lead to wholeness where there has been cleavage, unity where there has been division.

Nevertheless, the profusion of references in Job to Isaiah and other passages undeniably connected with the exile and return makes it clear that although the writer is going a step further, he is modelling his message very closely on Israel's experience. It is not therefore that Job is an allegorical picture of Israel, as though the writer were apparently talking about a figure of the distant past, but in reality about his own contemporaries as a nation. It is rather that through the figure of Job he is making Israel an allegorical picture of everyman: or, to be more accurate, everyman, without regard to race, who is drawn into that lifelong dialogue with God for which the career of Jacob serves as the classic model.

We have already had to consider the question how far the book provides an answer to the problem of suffering, and here there is need only for a summary of our earlier findings. God does not in his speech to Job answer the question, 'What have I done to deserve this?' But in the Epilogue, there is an answer to the question, 'What purpose does suffering serve?' implied by the healthful effect of the whole drama upon Job's friends; and there is an answer in that while there is no explanation of undeserved suffering, there is ample compensation.

There are, of course, limitations in the portrait of Job's latter days. The most obvious is that in the end he died. The concept of resurrection is touched on in the dialogue, but it does not form any part of the writer's final solution to the problem of Job's suffering. There is wealth. In Job's sons, there is the kind of hope for the future which every Israelite dreamed of. In the names of his daughters, there is the aura of peace (in Jemimah), of fragrance (in Keziah) and of beauty (in Keren-Happuch).[2] The careful doubling of everything is perhaps a reference to Isaiah 40:2; over against Israel's double payment in punishment for all their sins, Job is now doubly rewarded for all his undeserved sufferings. Even his life-span is doubled so that instead of merely seeing the grandchildren normally allotted to the man who reaches three score years

---

[2] Jemimah means 'turtle-dove'; Keziah 'cinnamon'; Keren-Happuch, horn of antimony, i.e. eye-shadow, which was normally kept in a horn.

and ten, Job sees four generations of his descendants. But in the end, however full of days, he dies.

He dies. In a way this might seem an inevitable end, and one which calls for little comment. Everybody dies, and Job was no exception. However, the importance attached to his being spared the death which during his troubles seemed so certain raises the question why it should be regarded as so significant if it meant only the delay of death, however much happier the circumstances surrounding it in the end might have been. Thus the death of Job draws attention more clamantly than other deaths in the Old Testament to the fact that there is here an unsolved problem. The Old Testament does not present us with any satisfying answer to death, and this is highlighted by the irony that Job evades it only for a time.

But there is none the less, and without reading back into the book the whole biblical sequel, a pointer here to newness of life. The writer was well enough aware that those who reached the stage of debility and disease that Job had reached do not recover. It follows that though at the end the writer shies away from the resurrection he adumbrates earlier in the book, he is still hinting at it. For the vindication of Job is no less intended as a vindication of God himself. But if the book has to be read as a fairy story rather than a parable, where is the vindication of God in real life? If his saints go to their graves unvindicated, and that is the end of the story, is not Job's folly (in making just this suggestion) wisdom after all?

Another way of putting this is to say that the Book of Job with its idyllic end has something which the Old Testament conspicuously lacks. If one thinks of the writer (as we have argued one ought to think of him) composing this poem when the scriptural canon had already begun to crystallize, and had all but reached the finality which at last came down to us, this is a thought which might well have been in his own mind. For the Old Testament, as it closed, was a library without solutions, fraught with the unyielding problems of justice and history. The Book of Job does not read in its entirety like a plaintive essay in wishful thinking, but much more like a blueprint of what would ultimately emerge.

2 The place of Job in the Bible as a whole

This all leads to considering the further meaning which the book gathers when one looks at it with the hindsight of Christian vision. It was for the joy that was set before him that Jesus endured the cross. And to judge by the store which he set by the Old Testament in teaching his disciples about the resurrection, one may expect the Book of Job to have figured largely in that hope. For where else is the happy outcome of bitter suffering so explicitly taught as in these pages?

But there are a great number of common features which serve to link the experience of Job with that of Jesus. To begin with, the suffering was undeserved. If Job could be called 'perfect'—as he is at the outset—it was in a relative and derived way. But Jesus was perfect in his own right. Then there is the fact that for Jesus as for Job the bitterness lay especially in the way in which his own friends let him down. There are many parallels in the physical agony which they each suffered. And at the heart of it all for them both lay the question which gives this book its title, and Job his name, 'Where is my father?' To go further and draw a parallel between the redemptive character of the sufferings of Job and of Jesus must clearly be done with care, for fear of detracting from the unique saving work of the cross. Nevertheless, the very important part played by intercession both in the prelude to Jesus's sufferings and in the course of them certainly gains in meaning when it is set as the climax of a biblical series in which the intercession of Job for his friends has its place.

All these points, however, pale into insignificance beside the new dimension which the resurrection of Jesus gives to the restoration of Job. Without that, certainly, as we have seen, the book hints at more than it states. But without that, the death of Job, however mitigated by his ultimate long-lived prosperity, in the end poses the problem which nothing in the Old Testament resolves. In the light of the resurrection of Jesus, on the other hand, with all that it promises for his followers, the restoration of Job becomes indeed a foretaste of heaven, and a foretaste of that newness of life which begins on earth for those who, it may be, after something of the same dark night through which Job went, find peace with God. In one sense, Job is a type of Christ, since like him he was compensated for suffering which he had done nothing to deserve. But in another sense, he is simply the model for every believer, his encounter with God preparing the way for the richer experience now freely available for all in the dying love of Jesus and in the empty tomb, which, not being able to hold him, presents the fact of his restoration and the promise of ours.

3 The promise of hope for today

It is because one can look at the Book of Job through Christian eyes that it has its two distinct applications for our own day. Many for this reason on the one hand have been able to read it in the face of death and find in it a comfort undisturbed either by the fact that Job was spared and physically restored or by the fact that in the end he too died. They need not expect the kind of miraculous reversal which Job experienced, provided that the book can speak realistically of a God who, however silent now, however apparently inactive, will at length stir himself to action. Job's restoration speaks to them of their resurrection. His paradise on earth faintly foreshadows what awaits them in heaven, beggaring all description.

But on the other hand the Book of Job has a message not only for those who are literally lying on their deathbeds. Job's predicament with its many facets stands for a wide variety of situations in which a human being feels that he is in a hopeless position. There may be nothing imaginary about this. The bankruptcy may be real and literal. So may the prison, or the storm, or the famine, or the fog, or the mountain, or the fire, or the instruments of torture. There is a countless register of plights in which a believer may well find himself, and from which he sees no possible way of escape. The Book of Job is a guarantee that the God who has apparently closed all doors will sometime, somehow, open one. Of course our philosophical friend will say cynically, 'Ah, yes; but the door is most often the door of death.' We cannot evade his cynicism. We have to learn our basic Christianity well enough to be able to retort that if so, that is the best door of all, since, as Paul put it, to be with Christ is far better (Phil. 1:23). But the truth is that death does not come as soon as we expect. God is forever opening the most unlikely doors to Christians who have seen themselves at the end of the road. The Book of Job does not name the door which God will open. But it promises one.

On the other hand, the bankruptcy may be imaginary. Psychiatrists know well enough that men with abundant financial resources can imagine themselves destitute. And every other physical predicament mentioned above can have its counterpart in a disease of the soul. A man can be lost in spite of knowing exactly where he is. The Book of Job does not say to such a person, 'You are not really lost'. It does not say, 'All your problems are imaginary'. It does not argue about the nature of our predicament at all. It simply says, 'Just as there was an end to the tunnel for Job, so there will be an end to the tunnel for you.' In the end there is an answer.

But for most of us most of the time, life is not a matter of grappling either with imminent death or with pathological depression. The kind of problems we face are not those which need to be taken to a doctor or a psychiatrist. They are nonetheless real and pressing. We have our hopeless situations. But they are not hopeless in the sense that death hangs over us. They are hopeless because we can see no way of bringing about a satisfying solution. They are situations in which we are inclined to say, 'We shall just have to live with it.' It stinks. It is hellish. It is offensively ugly. But nothing can be done, we tend to think.

The Book of Job does not encourage us to come grudgingly to terms with intractable problems. Difficulties with one's children, with one's marriage partner, or one's relatives; people in the church, or people at work—these are the stuff of which life is made up. But the Book of Job does not say, 'You have to grin and bear it'. It says that in the end, God will act in the situation. The solution may not be what we expect. It may come, as for Job, out of the whirlwind. But it is wrong to give up hope of an answer. Paul had a thorn which he asked God to remove, and the ultimate answer was, 'My grace is sufficient' (2 Cor. 12:9). Again, cynicism has its construction to put upon that. But the temptation to cynicism has to be resisted. As he gave Job three daughters, God will give a fragrance to what stinks, he will bring peace into what is hellish, and some form of beauty into the ugliest situation. Transformation may be brought about at the level of our attitude, perhaps. But transformation is what the Book of Job invites us perseveringly to expect.

And the transformation does not depend on our previous behaviour. Indeed it may well arise out of the same kind of experience as Job's. We rage at God. But he can take it. Afterwards he is still the same. This is one way of looking at the cross. Man does his worst to God. But afterwards God presents himself afresh, with an offer of peace. The Father whom we cry out to as irretrievably lost is not lost. 'Where is my Father?' He is still there; not only in spite of the sufferings which cast doubt in our minds about his reality, but in spite of those hostile reactions of ours which we imagine must finalize the breach. 'Where is my Father?' In the end he was still there for Job. The New Testament expansion of this makes it all the clearer that he is still there for us.

<u>Other publications by the same author</u>:

Contributor to the IVF New Bible Dictionary 1962

Towards a united church, Editor, MRF 1964

Studying God's Word, Editor, IVP 1972

What warmed John Wesley's heart?
          Daystar Press, Ibadan 1972

Seven steps to the cross, Daystar Press, Ibadan 1973

The teaching of the Old Testament,
          Scripture Union/ CLC 1984

God's watchman in Babylon, Paternoster 1984.

———————————

INDEX OF SCRIPTURE REFERENCES

INDEX OF MODERN AUTHORS